The Sources and Structures of
James Joyce's "Oxen"

Studies in Modern Literature, No. 15

A. Walton Litz, General Series Editor

Consulting Editor for Titles on James Joyce
Professor of English
Princeton University

Other Titles in This Series

The Sources and Structures of
James Joyce's "Oxen"

by
Robert Janusko

UMI RESEARCH PRESS
Ann Arbor, Michigan

I am grateful to the editors of Viking Press and to The Society of Authors as the literary representative of the Estate of James Joyce and Joyce Estate and The Joyce Archive, Garland Publishing, New York, U.S.A. for permission to quote from *A Portrait of the Artist as a Young Man, Critical Writings, Dubliners, Exiles, Finnegan's Wake,* and *Letters of James Joyce Vols. 1–3.* I am also grateful for permission to quote from the following works:

The Argument of Ulysses by Stanley Sultan. Copyright 1964. Reprinted by permission of Stanley Sultan.

James Joyce and the Making of Ulysses by Frank Budgen. Copyright 1960. Reprinted by permission of Indiana University Press.

Ulysses by James Joyce. Copyright 1914, 1918 by Margaret Caroline Anderson and renewed 1942, 1946 by Nora Joseph Joyce. Reprinted by permission of Random House, Inc.

James Joyce by Richard Ellman. Copyright 1959. Reprinted by permission of Oxford University Press, New York.

From *Signs and Symbols in Christian Art* by George Ferguson. Copyright 1954 and renewed by The Samuel H. Kress Foundation. Reprinted by permission of Oxford Univeristy Press, Inc.

Produced and distributed by
UMI Research Press
an imprint of
University Microfilms International
Ann Arbor, Michigan 48106

Library of Congress Cataloging in Publication Data

Janusko, Robert.
    The sources and structures of James Joyce's "Oxen".

    (Studies in modern literature ; no. 15)
    Revision of thesis (Ph.D.)–Kent State University, 1967.
    Bibliography: p.
    Includes index.
    1. Joyce, James, 1882-1941. Ulysses–Sources. 2. Joyce, James, 1882-1941–Technique. I. Title. II. Series.
    PR6019.O9U6586 1983   823'.912   83-6984
    ISBN 0-8357-1424-1

...What do you think Vulgariano did but study with stolen fruit how cutely to copy all their various styles of signature so as one day to utter an epical forged cheque on the public for his own private profit....

Finnegans Wake

Contents

Acknowledgments

Among those to whom I am indebted for encouraging my interest in Joyce and for contributing to the writing of this book are Bernard Benstock, under whose watchful guidance the original version of this study was written; Phillip Herring, whose correspondence on the problems surrounding Joyce's notes has proved invaluable; Weldon Thornton and Alan Cohn, who graciously shared with me typescript versions of their research on the "Oxen" many years ago; Joseph Prescott, whose generous encouragement and advice has been most helpful; and A. Walton Litz, who, in *The Art of James Joyce,* provided the clue that led me into the "Oxen" and who has now made possible the publication of my findings.

I also wish to thank R.D. Stock for his contribution to this study.

1

Introduction

At 10 P.M., on June 16, 1904, Leopold Bloom, the Ulysses of James Joyce's novel, visits the National Maternity hospital on Holles Street to inquire about an old friend, Mrs. Mina Purefoy, who has been in labor for three days. In the hospital he is approached by a young medical student, who invites him to a drinking-bout in the common room of the hospital. It is there, at the party, that Bloom, the bourgeois advertising salesman, finally confronts the young poet, Stephen Dedalus, the Telemachus of *Ulysses*. It is to this meeting, and to its subsequent effects on both Stephen and Bloom, that the action of the entire novel is directed. To portray this encounter Joyce produced a stylistic tour de force: a series of parodies of English literary styles, from the Anglo-Saxon of Aelfric to the Americanisms of the twentieth-century revivalist John Alexander Dowie, integrated with references to an episode in Homer's *Odyssey* and with the stages of growth of the human embryo.

Joyce began writing the "Oxen of the Sun" in February, 1920. In a letter dated the twenty-fifth of that month he confided to Harriet Shaw Weaver that the "Oxen of the Sun" was "the most difficult episode in an odyssey, I think, both to interpret and to execute...."[1] However difficult the task that Joyce had set for himself, by May of the same year he was able to inform Frank Budgen that "The oxen of the bloody bleeding sun are finished."[2]

Although Budgen was not with Joyce while he was writing the "Oxen," he does provide, in his book, *James Joyce and the Making of Ulysses*, a description of Joyce's usual method of gathering material for his novel:

In one of the richest pages of *Ulysses* Stephen, on the sea shore, communing with himself and tentatively building with words, calls for his tablets. These should have been library slips, acquired by the impecunious and ingenious poet from the library counter. On that occasion he had forgotten to provide himself with this convenient writing material, and was forced to use the fag-end of Mr. Deasy's letter. As far as concerns the need for tablets, the self-portrait was still like, only in Zurich Joyce was never without them. And they were not library slips, but little writing blocks specially made for the waistcoat pocket. At intervals, alone or in conversation, seated or walking, one of these tablets was produced, and a word or two scribbled on it at lightning speed as ear or memory served his turn. No one knew how all this material was given place in the completed pattern of his work, but from time to time in Joyce's flat one caught glimpses of a few of those big orange-coloured envelopes that are one of the glories of Switzerland, and these I always took to be storehouses of building material.[3]

Budgen was correct in assuming that the envelopes in Joyce's apartment were "storehouses of building material," and much has been learned about what they contained. The words scribbled on the writing blocks were sorted out and transferred to large sheets of paper, each sheet containing material for a specific portion of *Ulysses*. As Joyce used a word or phrase he crossed it off with a colored pencil, indicating that he had found a place for it in his novel. The notesheets for the last seven episodes of *Ulysses* are still extant, having been sent in 1938 by Paul Leon to Harriet Shaw Weaver, who deposited them in the British Museum. A. Walton Litz has arranged them according to the chapters to which they pertain, and in 1961 he published his description of the notesheets, showing how Joyce used these notes to thicken the texture of his work, a process which began in the last chapters of *Ulysses* and reached its culmination in the densities of *Finnegans Wake*.[4] Phillip Herring has since transcribed the sheets (no easy task as anyone who has ever tried to read Joyce's handwriting can attest), indicating where the notes appear in the printed text of *Ulysses*.[5] The present study complements the work done by Litz and Herring, tracing the entries on the "Oxen" notesheets back to the works from which Joyce copied characteristic words and phrases for his parodies of literary styles, and using the embryological characteristics on the sheets, together with the divisions of the "Oxen" manuscript at the Lockwood Memorial Library, to determine the nine-month structure of the chapter.[6]

Although Budgen did not know how Joyce used all of his building materials, he did know how the "Oxen of the Sun" was being constructed. On March 20, 1920, Joyce wrote him the letter outlining his plans for the chapter which has become the basis for all "Oxen" scholarship:

Am working hard at *Oxen of the Sun,* the idea being the crime committed against fecundity by sterilizing the act of coition. Scene, lying-in hospital. Technique: a nine-parted episode without divisions introduced by a Sallustian-Tacitean prelude (the unfertilized ovum), then by way of earliest English alliterative and monosyllabic and Anglo-Saxon ("Before born the babe had bliss. Within the womb he won worship." "Bloom dull dreamy heard: in held hat stony staring") then by way of Mandeville ("there came forth a scholar of medicine that men clepen etc") then Malory's *Morte d'Arthur* ("but that franklin Lenehan was prompt ever to pour them so that at the least way mirth should not lack"), then the Elizabethan chronicle style ("about that present time young Stephen filled all cups"), then a passage solemn, as of Milton, Taylor, Hooker, followed by a choppy Latin-gossipy bit, style of Burton-Browne, then a passage Bunyanesque ("the reason was that in the way he fell in with a certain whore whose name she said is Bird in the hand") after a diarystyle bit Pepys-Evelyn ("Bloom sitting snug with a party of wags, among them Dixon jun., Ja. Lynch, Doc. Madden and Stephen D. for a languor he had before and was now better, he having dreamed tonight a strange fancy and Mistress Purefoy there to be delivered, poor body, two days past her time and the midwives hard put to it, God send her quick issue") and so on through Defoe-Swift and Steele-Addison-Sterne and Landor-Pater-Newman until it ends in a frightful jumble of Pidgin English, nigger English, Cockney, Irish, Bowery slang and broken doggerel. This progression is also linked back at each part subtly with some foregoing episode of the day and, besides this, with the natural stages of development in the embryo and the periods of faunal evolution in general. The double-thudding Anglo-Saxon motive recurs from time to time ("Loth to move from Horne's house") to give the sense of the hoofs of oxen. Bloom is the spermatozoon, the hospital the womb, the nurse the ovum, Stephen the embryo.

How's that for high?[7]

It has been too high for some of Joyce's readers who feel that the "Oxen of the Sun" is a most difficult episode to interpret and seem almost ready to execute Joyce for having violated their aesthetic standards by writing it. Those who object to the chapter admit that it is a brilliant technical achievement, but complain that such a tour de force, interweaving the narrative with Homeric correspondences, parodies of English literary styles, and references to the growth of the human embryo, not only obscures the narrative but is "out of proportion to its function."[8] There are of course guides which have been provided for this chapter, to help the reader unravel the separate strands of which it is composed and, hopefully, to enable him to see the design of the whole and to soothe offended aesthetic sensibilities. In 1930 Stuart Gilbert, with Joyce's help, wrote the first, and as yet unsurpassed, full-scale examination of the chapter, indicating the Homeric parallels and some of the embryological references, and identifying the parodies.[9] Nineteen years later, A. M. Klein, building on the work of Gilbert and the letter from Joyce to Budgen, attempted to delineate the nine months of gestation, the periods of evolution, and the links between the "Oxen" and the preceding chapters.[10]

Klein's article, although usually described as "brilliant," has added more to the confusion about the chapter than to an understanding of it, and has not won unqualified acclaim. Hugh Kenner, referring the "curious reader" to Klein's "labyrinthine schematization" of the chapter, warns that "It probably isn't necessary to suppose that Joyce was quite so fantastic a mathematician as Mr. Klein would like to believe."[11] Ellsworth Mason, admitting that Klein provides some insight into the details of the chapter, believes that "Mr. Klein's article on the 'Oxen' is demonstrably wrong," but does not support this assertion.[12] J. S. Atherton states, "Anyone following in Klein's steps must be grateful to him," but concludes, "Joyce uses the

details he inserts more light-heartedly than Klein could believe and pro-
duces effects funnier than Klein realized."[13]

The extent to which Klein is wrong in his division of the nine months
of the "Oxen," on which his schematization and stages of evolution are
based, will be demonstrated in more detail in chapter three below.

Armed with Weldon Thornton's *Allusions,* Don Gifford's and Robert
J. Seidman's *Notes,* and one or more of the many studies of the "Oxen,"
a reader should have no greater problem bringing the narrative of this
chapter into the light than any other chapter of *Ulysses.*[14] The linguistic
difficulties encountered are, after all, no more formidable than those an
undergraduate student of Chaucer is expected to surmount. The Homeric
correspondences are similar to those found throughout the book, as are the
"links" with other chapters, the repetition of motives being one of Joyce's
major unifying techniques. The use of embryological correspondences is
merely a mechanical device, like the "tumescence-detumescence" of "Nau-
sicaa" or the *"fuga per canonem"* of the "Sirens," used by Joyce to impose
some order on his material. An extensive knowledge of embryology is not
necessary to understand the "Oxen"; as will be shown below in chapter
three of this study, it may even be a hindrance, since Joyce was rather free
in his handling of the characteristics of prenatal growth. Since no references to the periods of faunal evolution appear on the notesheets, I surmise
that Joyce abandoned his intention to incorporate them in his text and do
not believe that it would serve any useful purpose to distort the sense of his
words in order to find them.

It may, however, increase the understanding and enjoyment of this
episode to see the manner in which Joyce wrote this chapter and the specific passages on which he drew to construct his parodies. The value of
identifying the parodies has often been called into question. Richard M.
Kain, for example, lists in his study only the more important of them "for
what they are worth."[15] It must be admitted that a list of identifications, by
itself, is not worth much, since there are perhaps few readers who are well
enough steeped in each of the authors parodied to fully appreciate the
entire series of imitations. At most, one or two parodies are usually singled
out as especially brilliant, Dickens or Carlyle, for example, because, I
suspect, of the reader's previous familiarity with their style.

Another significant consideration is that put forth by Harry Levin,
"For what organic reason, if any, must Lyly represent the foetus in the
third month, and Goldsmith in the sixth? And what's Bunyan to Mrs.
Purefoy, or Mrs. Purefoy to Junius?"[16] I can only answer that this is the
wrong way to bring these questions to the chapter. None of the authors
parodied in the "Oxen" represents the fetus per se; they represent stages in
the chronological development of English literary history. To insist upon a

complete identification between the embryological structure of this chapter and literary history would place both the reader and Joyce in a rather awkward position. The fetus, by its very nature, grows to perfection in the womb as it approaches its final end, birth as a human being, each stage in its development being an improvement over the last. In literary evaluation, however, only the most extreme modernist would claim that contemporary literature is superior, simply because it is chronologically later than what has gone before. It is doubtful that Joyce would have exalted the prose style of Dickens over Swift and Burke, or that of John Alexander Dowie over Newman.

Although there is no necessary organic correlation between most of the authors parodied and the months in which they appear, the placement of authors is not completely fortuitous. In the sixth month, for example, the fact that the scrotum of the male fetus is empty is announced in the voice of two writers whose styles are anything but emasculated, Defoe and Swift. Defoe describes Lenehan "with a bare tester in his purse" (*U,* 398.25–26) and with "naked pockets" (*U,* 399.10).[17] In the "bull" discussion, the voice of Swift tells the tale of "farmer Nicholas that was a eunuch" who sent to Ireland the bull of Laudabiliter, which was "properly gelded by a college of doctors, who were no better off than himself" (*U,* 399.41–400.01). Rather than using these writers to represent a month in the development of the fetus, Joyce in this instance achieves a comic effect by letting them comment on a specific feature of prenatal growth which is incongruous with their own roles in the development of literary history.

In like manner, Bunyan may be nothing to Mrs. Purefoy, but he was the voice of God thundering at the vices and snares of the Commonwealth and Restoration, and he appears in *Ulysses* to condemn both the "whore Bird-in-the-Hand (which was within all foul plagues, monsters and a wicked devil)" (*U,* 396.07–08) and the earlier stage of the conversation about the "delights amorous" (*U,* 393.16) of the age of Beaumont and Fletcher. Mrs. Purefoy may be nothing to Junius, but it was Junius who exposed the hypocrisy of eighteenth-century England and it is Junius who exposes the hypocrisy of Bloom, "a censor of morals, a very pelican in his piety, who did not scruple, oblivious of the ties of nature, to attempt illicit intercourse with a female domestic drawn from the lowest strata of society" (*U,* 409.33–34).

Rather than beginning with the name of an author and comparing him to the month in which he occurs, or trying to relate authors and particular characters at random, a more fruitful approach is to start with the narrative, to see what the action is and what words (including the wealth of puns) are used to express it. Then the reader can begin to ask why certain words from a certain author are used to describe a specific action or to express the thought of a particular digression. It is also at this point that individual embryological characteristics, not vague "months," can be related to their proper function in the texture of a specific passage. The entries on the notesheets enable the reader to perform this task with some degree of accuracy, for it is there that one finds Joyce's vocabulary lists and fetal characteristics, and it is to the correlation of this material with the narrative that the following chapters of this study are devoted.

2

Narrative and Themes

Stuart Gilbert has explained the relationship between the slaying of the oxen of the sun in Homer's *Odyssey* and "the crime committed against fecundity by sterilizing the act of coition" by pointing out that Trinacria, now known as Sicily, in addition to being the home of Helios, the sun god, was also the site of an Aphroditic cult, "whose *Aphrodision* was famous for its...(phallic and triangular), sexual emblems of Phoenician origin."[1] Joyce fused the two Trinacrian deities so that any crime against the sun would also be a crime against sex, and with good reason. Both the sun and the sexual act bring life into the world; man could not long survive in a state of darkness or sterility.

But even without Gilbert's explanation, it is not difficult to find in the sun an image of procreation and fecundity. Copernicus, for example, in his *De Revolutionibus,* assigns to the sun a most important place in his cosmos:

> In the middle of all sits Sun enthroned. In this most beautiful temple could we place this luminary in any better position from which he can illuminate the whole at once? He is rightly called the Lamp, the Mind, the Ruler of the Universe; Hermes Trismegistus names him the Visible God, Sophocles' Electra calls him the All-seeing. So the Sun sits as upon a royal throne ruling his children the planets which circle round him. The Earth has the Moon at her service. As Aristotle says, in his *On the Generation of Animals,* the Moon has the closest relationship with the Earth. Meanwhile the Earth conceives by the Sun, and becomes pregnant with an annual rebirth.[2]

The sun is also a traditional Christian symbol for Christ, the Son of God,

> this interpretation being based on the prophecy of Malachi 4:2: "But unto you that fear my name shall the sun of righteousness arise with healing in his wings." The sun and the moon are used as attributes of the Virgin Mary, referring to the "woman clothed with the sun, and the moon under her feet" (Revelation 12:1). The sun and the moon are often represented in scenes of the Crucifixion to indicate the sorrow of all creation at the death of Christ. St. Thomas Aquinas is sometimes depicted with a sun on his breast.[3]

The "Dumb Ox" of scholastic metaphysics, of whose works Stephen is so fond, is as important for his formulation of the Roman Catholic doctrine of transubstantiation as he is for providing Stephen with a basis for his aesthetics, both of which achievements are alluded to in this chapter. But the ox has served other functions in Christian symbology than providing Aquinas with a nickname:

> The ox, a sacrificial animal of the Jews, was often used in Renaissance painting to represent the Jewish nation. It is also used as a symbol of patience and strength. Almost invariably, the ox and the ass appear together in paintings of the Nativity.... In the writings of some of the early Christian fathers, the ox is accepted as a symbol of Christ, the true sacrifice. The symbol is similarly used to represent all who patiently bear their yoke while laboring in silence for the good of others. The winged ox is the attribute of St. Luke because of his emphasis upon the sacrificial aspects of our Lord's atonement as well as upon His divine priesthood.[4]

Add to this the fact that St. Luke was a physician, and the complex of Homeric and Christian associations attached to the sun and the ox which can profitably be brought to this chapter is, if not complete, at least rich.[5] The sun is the source of light and life, both physical and intellectual. It is paternal and, by impregnating the earth, brings about a cyclical rebirth. It is also the Son who rises "with healing in his wings," the Word made flesh at the Incarnation and reincarnated by transubstantiation at the consecration of the Mass. The ox is both Christ and the patient, strong, hardworking animal present at the Nativity. It represents the Jewish nation, and Bloom is a Jew. It is the animal of sacrifice and atonement; as Christ it is both priest and victim. That St. Luke was a physician is perhaps one reason the "art" of the "Oxen" is medicine.

The slaying of the sacred oxen takes many forms in this chapter: sins against the light of intellect, of spirit, of artistic inspiration, labor, and creation; against maternity, paternity, the Son, the Holy Ghost, the Jew. If the Church is the spouse of Christ, and if the vicar of Christ on earth is a "eunuch" (*U,* 399.42), the Church is both sinned against and sinning, sterile and dark. But there are also occasional flashes of light in this sinladen gloom: Mina Purefoy has her baby; the "votaries of levity" now sinning against the light may someday, when they grow up, blossom into "exemplary practitioners of an art which most men anywise eminent have esteemed the noblest" (*U,* 408.40–42). Bloom has a vision in which "the everlasting bride, harbinger of the daystar, the bride, ever virgin" (*U,* 414.30–31) rises up to blaze "Alpha, a ruby and triangled sign upon the forehead of Taurus" (*U,* 414.40–41). Rain falls on Dublin with its promise of renewing life in the parched soil. When the revelers leave the hospital, "The air without is impregnated with raindew moisture, life essence celestial, glistering on Dublin stone there under star-shiny *coelum*. God's air, the Allfather's air, scintillant circumambiant cessile air" (*U,* 423.20–23). The chapter ends with the announcement that "Elijah is coming washed in the Blood of the Lamb" (*U,* 428.14–15), in the language of Alexander J. Christ Dowie, the American evangelist. Although America is west of Ireland, and to go west is traditionally to follow the setting sun, to die, America is also the new world. When Theodore Purefoy is praised, it is because "Thou sawest thy America, thy lifetask, and didst charge to cover like the transpontine bison" (*U,* 424.06–07), recalling Theodore Roosevelt, founder of the "Bull moose" party, who led the Rough Riders in the charge at San Juan Hill, and who was president of the United States in 1904. An evangelical voice from America is a voice from a new-found land, a crude and bawling cry that suggests a new beginning.[6]

The opposite, yet complementary, themes of life and death are present throughout the chapter, as they are throughout *Ulysses*. There is also, for Bloom at any rate, a general movement from death to life; in the morning he attends a funeral, in the evening a birth. That the birth occurs eleven hours after the funeral, and in the eleventh chapter of the "Odyssey" section of *Ulysses* may be no accident. The number eleven was for Joyce the number of rebirth, the number of renewal after the completion of a decade.[7]

To show how Joyce plays with the connotations of the ox and sun images, and the variations of the life and death, fertility and sterility themes to which they give rise, and to demonstrate in small measure the "links" with previous chapters, I offer the following explication, by no means complete, of the "Oxen." Although no summary can hope to capture the humor of Joyce's writing, I believe that a clear understanding of the narrative is a necessary preliminary to any discussion of the function of the embryological characteristics and, especially, of the parodies of English literary styles.

The first three paragraphs of the chapter provide a composition of place and of purpose. We are invited, in Gaelic, English, and Latin, to go south to Holles Street. Following the invocation to the sun god to send "quickening and wombfruit" (*U,* 383.03–06), the newborn manchild is elevated and praised in the voice of the midwife, "Hoopsa, boyaboy, hoopsa!" (*U,* 383.07–08).

The next four paragraphs give a short history of the medical profession in Ireland, the founding of the lying-in hospital, and a description of Mina Purefoy's admission there. We are told that only a truly ignorant man would fail to realize that a nation's prosperity is most evident in the solicitude it shows for child-bearing mothers and for the continuance of the race. Any intelligent man can perceive that a society's exterior, material splendor often disguises an inner corruption, and it behoves him to remind his fellows of the command to increase and multiply and of the promise of abundance to follow as a reward for obedience to this evangel. It is no wonder, then, that the Celts, who admired all worthy things, promoted the study of the art of medicine and honored its practitioners, the greatest of whom were "the O'Shiels, the O'Hickeys, the O'Lees" (*U,* 384.03), who flourished even before the Norman conquest.[8] Realizing the importance of childbirth, the Celts built lying-in hospitals, providing care for both rich and poor. It is to one of these hospitals that Mina Purefoy has come to be delivered, and it is there "that she by them suddenly to be about to be cherished had been begun she felt" (*U,* 384.28–30). Even though her child is not yet born, all is in readiness for his appearance and all possible care has been taken to facilitate his birth and to comfort his mother.

This is the scene into which wayfaring Bloom is introduced. When he first heard that Mrs. Purefoy was in labor that morning from Mrs. Breen, "His heavy pitying gaze absorbed her news. His tongue clacked in compassion" (*U,* 159.07–08). It is the same compassion that brings him to the hospital, "Stark ruth of man his errand" (*U,* 385.05). He has a more realistic picture of Mina's labor than that presented in the introduction to this chapter: "Three days imagine groaning on a bed with a vinegared handkerchief round her forehead, her belly swollen out! Phew! Dreadful simply! Child's head too big: forceps. Doubled up inside her trying to butt its way out blindly, groping for the way out. Kill me that would" (*U,* 161.22–26). Unlike the medical students, who have become inured to such sights, Bloom is able to sympathize with "women's woe in the travail that they have of motherhood" (*U,* 386.18–19).

In the description of the hospital appears the first reference to the Incarnation of Christ, "bring forth bairns hale so God's angel to Mary quoth" (*U,* 385.08–09), a theme which recurs throughout the chapter and reaches its culmination in "the vigilant watch of shepherds and of angels about a crib in Bethlehem of Juda long ago" (*U,* 422.33–34). Just as Gerty MacDowell in the previous chapter is ironically identified with the Virgin, Mina Purefoy suggests the childbearing mother of God. The miracle of Christ's incarnation, Joyce seems to imply, is no more wonderful than any incarnation, any embodiment of a soul.

Of the two nurses on duty that night, it is Miss Callan who answers the door and, seeing a flash of lightning in the western sky, invites Bloom to come in out of the impending rain. They stand in the hall, renewing their former acquaintance. Bloom asks her pardon for not greeting her once at a civic meeting; she notices his mourning clothes and is relieved when he tells her that it is not a close relative that has died. Bloom asks her about Doctor O'Hare, whose coat he had once noticed her brushing (cf.

U, 373.14-15), and she answers that "O'Hare Doctor in heaven was" (*U,* 385.33-34), having died of cancer almost three years ago.

At this announcement a voice intrudes, reminding "everyman" to remember his "last end that is thy death" (*U,* 386.05). Although this is a chapter on birth, the beginning of life, it is not unrelated to death, the last end of life, for birth is the beginning of death just as death is the beginning of "undeathliness" (*U,* 386.01). The close connection between conception, birth and death is reiterated often in *Ulysses.* Walking along Sandymount Strand, Stephen thinks, "Oomb, allwombing tomb" (*U,* 48.08). At Paddy Dignam's funeral Bloom thinks "Love among the tombstones. Romeo. Spice of pleasure. In the midst of death we are in life. Both ends meet" (*U,* 108.15-16). After the grave diggers cover the coffin, one of them "coiled the coffinband. His navelcord" (*U,* 112.29-30). On the way to the cemetery an old woman peeks out of a window at the funeral procession; "Extraordinary the interest they take in a corpse. Glad to see us go we give them such trouble coming" (*U,* 87.17). Bloom thinks about Dixon who dressed his bee sting at the Mater Misericordia, "Our Lady's Hospice for the dying. Deadhouse handy underneath" (*U,* 97.24-25). Dixon has now "gone over to the lying-in hospital they told me. From one extreme to the other" (*U,* 97.29-30). That "every man that is born of woman...as he came naked forth from his mother's womb so naked shall he wend him at the last for to go as he came" (*U,* 386.06-08) is anticipated in Bloom's "Nature. Washing child, washing corpse" (*U,* 373.07-08). It is the woman's function in Bloom's world to bear, bring forth and bury; man comes forth from an earthly mother and returns to Mother Earth. This eternal round might be called the feminine principle of continuity in *Ulysses.* The paternal principle is what Bloom is lacking; listening to Simon Dedalus talk about Stephen at the funeral, Bloom thinks, "Noisy selfwilled man. Full of his son. He is right. Something to hand on. If little Rudy had lived. See him grow up. Hear his voice in the house. Walking beside Molly in an Eton suit. My son. Me in his eyes. Strange feeling it would be. From me. Just a chance" (*U,* 89.02-06). This is Bloom's, and perhaps also Joyce's, substitute for a life beyond death; to live on in one's progeny rather than surviving as an individual consciousness. Many of the attitudes expressed in this chapter towards the importance of procreation and birth are evidently those of Joyce himself. Richard Ellmann, in his biography of Joyce, reports that a few years after the birth of his son Giorgio (July 27, 1905) Joyce

said to his sister Eva, "The most important thing that can happen to a man is the birth of a child."... In his Paris Notebook Joyce quoted prominently a sentence of Aristotle, "The most natural act for living beings which are complete is to produce other beings like themselves and thereby to participate as far as they may in the eternal and the divine." Many years later Joyce said to Louis Gillet, "I can't understand households without children. I see some with dogs, gimcracks. Why are they alive? To leave nothing behind, not to survive yourself – how sad!"[9]

Joyce's comment to Gillet is repeated in the congratulation of Theodore Purefoy at the end of the "Oxen": "Dost envy Darby Dullman there with his Joan? A canting jay and a rheumeyed curdog is all their progeny. Pshaw, I tell thee! He is a mule, a dead gasterpod, without vim or stamina, not worth a cracked kreutzer. Copulation without population! No, say I! Herod's slaughter of the innocents were the truer name" (*U,* 423.35–40). Bloom is not this enthusiastic about unrestrained procreation. Although he shows great reverence for birth, he is too prudent and considerate to expect his wife to bear as many children as has "Poor Mrs. Purefoy! Methodist husband. Method in his madness.... Hardy annuals he presents her with. Saw him out at the Three Jolly Topers marching along bareheaded and his eldest boy carrying one in a marketnet. The squallers. Poor thing! Then having to give breast year after year all hours of the night" (*U,* 161.01 –10). Bloom's ideal state would provide material security at birth for all its citizens: "out of all the taxes give every child born five quid at compound interest up to twentyone, five per cent is a hundred shillings and five tiresome pounds, multiply by twenty decimal system, encourage people to put by money save hundred and ten and a bit twentyone years want to work it out on paper come to a tidy sum, more than you think" (*U,* 161.34–40). Bloom embodies the bourgeois virtues of kindness, consideration, prudence, thrift, a concern for "that exterior splendour" of society which "may be the surface of a downwardtending lutulent reality" (*U,* 383.23–24). His attitude is the opposite of Richard Rowan's in *Exiles,* for whom "to take care for the future is to destroy hope and love in the world."[10]

The name Purefoy, fittingly taken from Dr. R. Damon Purefoy, a prominent Dublin obstetrician,[11] is not without significance in this regard. Literally, the name means "pure faith," reflecting the faith in the future of the race evidenced by the doctor who both keeps people alive and brings infants into the world, and by the proliferant Purefoys who have taken literally the "prophecy of abundance" (*U,* 383.37) and produced so many children without being oversolicitous for their future welfare. This opposition of faith and reasoned planning is graphically presented in the black mass in "Circe": "*On the altarstone Mrs. Mina Purefoy, goddess of unreason, lies naked, fettered, a chalice resting on her swollen belly*" (*U,* 599.12–14). It is on her body that the mass is said, that the transubstantiation takes place and from which a "*blooddripping host*" (*U,* 599.25) is taken to be elevated, just as it is on her body that the act of faith is performed, in which the copulating couple call on God to perform another incarnation, and from which a blooddripping child will be taken to be elevated with cries of "Hoopsa, boyaboy, hoopsa!" That Joyce at least considered this interpretation of the sexual act is supported by a notesheet entry which was not crossed off, "Fucker obliges God to create."[12] Both acts are miraculous; both demand faith; both are degraded in the Dublin of *Ulysses*: the Mass by inversion, copulation not only by "sterilizing the act of coition," but also by the aura of sin with which it has often been invested by Roman Catholicism, reflected in Stephen's thoughts on the Strand: "Wombed in sin darkness I was too, made not begotten. By them, the man with my voice and my eyes and a ghostwoman with ashes on her breath. They clasped and sundered, did the coupler's will" (*U*, 38.10–13). It is ironic that those characters in *Ulysses* who contribute most to the prosperity of Catholic Dublin are the anti-clerical Simon Dedalus, the drunken, dead Paddy Dignam, and Theodore Purefoy, a Methodist.

As Bloom and nurse Callan stand talking in the hall, they are approached by Dixon who is on duty at the hospital that night. Dixon invites Bloom to join him in a drinking-bout in the common-room of the hospital. Bloom at first demurs, but at Dixon's insistence, enters "the castle for to rest him for a space being sore of limb after many marches environing in divers lands and sometimes venery" (*U*, 386.42–387.02). Although "childe Leopold's" venery may have been hunting, Bloom's is more akin to the pursuit of Venus. Mulligan has seen "His pale Galilean eyes...upon her mesial groove. Venus Kallipyge. O, the thunder of those loins! *The god pursuing the maiden hid*" (*U*, 201.10–12). A more immediate cause of Bloom's need for rest is the fact that Gerty MacDowell made no attempt to hide her maidenhead that evening on the beach, provoking Bloom's masturbation and subsequent detumescence, "Exhausted that female has me" (*U*, 381.26).

The table is next described in fabulous terms, with knives, glasses, fish and ale. Dixon pours a drink for Bloom who, ever prudent, "voided the more part in his neighbour glass and his neighbour wist not of his wile" (*U*, 387.31–32). Nurse Callan asks the drinkers to "leave their wassailing" (*U*, 387.37) out of reverence for the laboring mother above, but is ignored.

Bloom spies Lenehan in the group and speaks to him, "or it be long too she will bring forth by God his bounty and have joy of her childing" (*U*, 388.03–05), but Lenehan, who has been drinking for quite a while and does not share Bloom's solicitude for Mrs. Purefoy, answers flippantly, "Expecting each moment to be her next" (*U*, 388.06–07). Lenehan has very little affection for Bloom this evening because he thinks that Bloom won one hundred shillings on the Ascot Gold Cup race, on which Lenehan bet unsuccessfully (*U*, 335.16–20). It was Lenehan who started the story at Barney Kiernan's earlier in the day that caused Bloom to be chased out with such indignity.

The names are then listed of those who are "there to be drunken an they might" (*U,* 388.17-18): Dixon, Lynch, Madden, Lenehan, Crotthers, Stephen, Costello, and Bloom. They are awaiting the appearance of Malachi Mulligan, who has been invited to a literary soiree at George Moore's, from which Stephen, who considers himself more a poet than Mulligan, has been excluded. The conversation turns to the problem of whether a doctor should attempt to save the life of a mother or of her child, if the survival of one depends on the death of the other. Stephen answers that even if both should die, "Both babe and parent now glorify their Maker, the one in limbo gloom, the other in purge fire. But, gramercy, what of those Godpossibled souls that we nightly impossibilise, which is the sin against the Holy Ghost, Very God, Lord and Giver of Life?" (*U,* 389.21-25). But Stephen's companions have drunken overmuch and refuse to consider their guilt, preferring to affirm the value of immediate gratification without concern for the results of their actions. Only Bloom and Stephen refuse to take part in the merriment, Bloom because of his compassion for "her that bare whoso she might be or wheresoever" (*U,* 389.41); Stephen because of his pride and his resentment against the Church which holds that "that earthly mother which was but a dam to bring forth beastly should die by canon" (*U,* 390.10-11), recalling the fact that Stephen's own mother is "beastly dead" (*U,* 8.20). His loss is too recent for him to speak of dying mothers with levity, as a purely academic problem.

The question is then put to Bloom, who answers that in "so seldom seen an accident it was good for that Mother Church belike at one blow had birth and death pence" (*U,* 390.19-21). If Stephen's answer has the "true scholastic stink," Bloom's has the smell of the practical materialist; both are in character.[13] Stephen is amused at Bloom's answer and avers that "he who stealeth from the poor lendeth to the Lord" (*U,* 390.24-25), words first spoken in the novel by Buck Mulligan before diving into the forty-foot hole for a swim that morning (*U,* 23.07). Stephen quotes Mulligan again, without benefit of footnote, in the discussion of Beaumont and Fletcher: "Thus, or words to that effect, said Zarathustra, sometime regius professor of French letters to the university of Oxtail" (*U,* 393.19-21), a combination of Mulligan's "Thus spake Zarathustra" (*U,* 23.07-08) and "Monsieur Moore...lecturer on French letters to the youth of Ireland" (*U,* 214.42-215.01). The pun on "French letters," both literature and contraceptive, does not speak highly of Moore's influence on the young Irish literati.

The talk about infant mortality and the sound of "the terrorcausing shrieking of shrill women in their labour" (*U,* 390.29-30) remind Bloom of his own son, Rudy, who died when he was only eleven days old. Just as in the "Hades" episode, when Simon Dedalus' talk brought Rudy (and what it might be like to have a son) to Bloom's mind, in the "Oxen" thoughts of Rudy cause Bloom to look upon Stephen and grieve for this prodigal son who "lived riotously with those wastrels and murdered his goods with whores" (*U,* 391.01–02).

Stephen fills the cups again with ale, and proposes a toast to the Pope. He parodies the consecration from the Mass and the Last Supper, saying that the ale is not his body, but his "soul's bodiment" (*U,* 391.10), his spirit.[14] He apparently lies about the source of his wealth, "two pound nineteen shilling that he had, he said, for a song which he writ" (*U,* 391.14–15), money which is probably left from the "Three twelve" (*U,* 30.06) he received from Mr. Deasy.[15]

With allusions to Blake and Yeats, "time's ruins build eternity's mansions. . . . Desire's wind blasts the thorntree but after it becomes from a bramblebush to be a rose upon the rood of time" (*U,* 391.18–21), Stephen restates the conception of the role of the artist that he developed in *A Portrait:* "a priest of the eternal imagination, transmuting the daily bread of experience into the radiant body of everliving life" (*P,* 221.14–16). His prophetic, Christlike function is indicated by "the words that shall not pass away" (*U,* 391.22–23), recalling Christ's prophecy of the destruction of Jerusalem, "Heaven and earth will pass away, but my words will not pass away" (Matthew 24:35). Talk of incarnation leads Stephen to the Incarnation of Christ and a mock theological problem, created only by a play on words: If Mary knew the Holy Ghost, in the Biblical sense, Christ's father was a pigeon and Joseph an archetypal cuckold; if she did not know Christ, she denied him as did Peter after Christ was taken prisoner by the Sanhedrin. This passage is reminiscent of the legalistic "curious questions" with which Stephen baited the rector in *A Portrait* (*P,* 106).

Costello responds to Stephen's speech by beginning to sing "a bawdy catch *Staboo Stabella* about a wench that was put in pod of a jolly swashbuckler" (*U,* 392.05–06), but is interrupted by nurse Quigley, who tries, as did Miss Callan before, to quiet the revelers. They all reprimand Costello, calling him "thou chuff, thou puny, thou got in the peasestraw, thou losel, thou chitterling, thou spawn of a rebel, thou dykedropt, thou abortion thou" (*U,* 392.19–21). Since this namecalling occurs in the third month of the chapter, it is interesting to note that, according to Ellmann, Joyce's wife Nora had suffered a miscarriage in 1908, while she was in the third month of her pregnancy. "She did not much mind losing the third child, but Joyce carefully examined the fetus, 'whose truncated existence,' he said to Stanislaus, 'I am probably the only one to regret.' This miscarriage helped to make Bloom's chief sorrow, in *Ulysses,* the death just after birth of his son Rudy."[16] It may have also influenced the writing of this passage.

After the tumult subsides, Dixon asks Stephen "why he had not cided to take friar's vows" (*U*, 392.29). He replies, parodying the religious vows of poverty, chastity, and obedience, "obedience in the womb, chastity in the tomb but involuntary poverty all his days" (*U*, 392.30–31); he will not serve, he cannot be chaste, but he is poor. Stephen at one time did consider becoming a priest, "wielding calmly and humbly the awful power of which the angels and saints stood in reverence" (*P*, 158.14–16), but when invited to join the Jesuits, declined, being "destined to learn his own wisdom apart from others or to learn the wisdom of others himself wandering among the snares of the world. The snares of the world were its ways of sin" (*P*, 162.09–13), and Stephen's sins are pride and lust. When Lenehan accuses him of besmirching "the lily virtue of a confiding female" (*U*, 392.33–34), he denies it, claiming to be, like Christ, "the eternal son and ever virgin" (*U*, 392.37). His reply signals an increase in merriment, and they all remind him of his exotic rite "for the disrobing and deflowering of spouses" (*U*, 392.39–40), which is no doubt considered obscene by those present, but is actually in keeping with the sacramental nature of copulation described earlier in this chapter. Stephen sings for them a song from the masque celebrating the nuptials of Amintor and Evadne in *The Maid's Tragedy* by Beaumont and Fletcher:

> To bed, to bed! Come, Hymen, lead the bride,
> And lay her by her husband's side;
>   Bring in the virgins every one,
>   That grieve to lie alone,
> That they may kiss while they may say a maid;
> To-morrow 't will be other kiss'd and said.
>   Hesperus, be long a-shining,
>   While these lovers are a-twining.[17]

What Stephen's auditors do not know, or choose to ignore, is that this song portends no joy in its original context. Amintor has jilted Aspatia, his first love, to marry Evadne, who is the mistress of the King and is marrying only to conceal her unholy alliance. Before the play is over, Evadne kills both the King and herself and Amintor kills Aspatia by mistake before committing suicide. The marriage is never even consummated. The song is ironic in *The Maid's Tragedy;* the allusion to it in the "Oxen" suggests that a like retribution may be visited upon the insensitive "juveniles amatory" in the common-room of the hospital.

Stephen's song is followed by a flurry of Elizabethan allusions. Stephen's remembrance that Beaumont and Fletcher "had but the one doxy between them" (*U*, 393.14–15) is a paraphrase of Aubrey's: "They lived together on the Banke side, not far from the Play-house, both bachelors; lay together; had one Wench in the house between them, which they did so

17

admire. . . ."[18] Several phrases are repeated from the "Scylla and Charybdis" chapter, which consists mainly of a discussion of Shakespeare: "Life ran very high in those days" (*U,* 393.16, 204.20–21); "professor of French letters" (*U,* 393.20–21, 214.42). "Greater love than this. . .no man hath that a man lay down his wife for his friend" (*U,* 393.17–19) recalls "a man who holds so tightly to what he calls his rights over what he calls his debts will hold tightly also to what he calls his rights over her whom he calls his wife" (*U,* 205.42–206.03). The "secondbest bed" (*U,* 203.41–42, 206.15), left by Shakespeare to his wife Ann, takes on added significance here when Stephen says "Bring a stranger within thy tower it will go hard but thou wilt have the secondbest bed" (*U,* 393.22–24), alluding to the fact that Haines has displaced him from his rightful place in the Martello tower. In the "Circe" episode this phrase is again used by Bella Cohen to Bloom, "You have made your secondbest bed and others must lie in it" (*U,* 543.20–21), a reference to Blazes Boylan's cuckolding of Bloom.

Stephen's reproach to Ireland, introduced by *"Orate fratres, pro memetipso"* (Pray brothers, for I myself, *U,* 393.24), a parody of the *Orate fratres* from the Offertory of the Mass (which is not answered "Amen"), seems to contain reproaches against Bloom's wife Molly and "Clan Milly," his daughter, as well as against the country which has betrayed Stephen. The "merchant of jalaps" (*U,* 393.32–33) suggests Haines, whose "old fellow made his tin by selling jalap to Zulus" (*U,* 7.10–11) and his country, "The imperial British State" (*U,* 20.34); "the Roman" (*U,* 393.33) suggests the Roman Catholic Church, the "crazy queen, old and jealous" (*U,* 20.30), Stephen's Italian master. The "Indian of dark speech" (*U,* 393.33–34) recalls the Theosophists, who had captivated the interest of the Irish literati. Together they constitute the political, religious and artistic surrender of Ireland and parallel the three denials of Christ by Peter. Ireland has left Stephen "alone for ever in the dark ways of my bitterness; and with a kiss of ashes hast thou kissed my mouth" (*U,* 393.40–41), recalling not only the "faint odour of wetted ashes" (*U,* 10.18) on his dead mother's breath in his dream, but also the "odour of ashpits and old weeds and offal" which hang around Joyce's stories in *Dubliners.*[19] Both mother and country are dead for Stephen, but they refuse to stay buried.

The darkness of bitterness, he continues, has not been alleviated by either the word of the Old Testament, "the wit of the septuagint" (*U,* 394.01), or the Word of the New, "for the Orient from on high which brake hell's gates visited a darkness that was foraneous" (*U,* 394.01–03). The prophecy of Zachary (Luke 1:78–79) cannot be fulfilled for Stephen because his darkness is more exquisite than that of the marketplace. Although "assuefaction minorates atrocities" (*U,* 394.06), the terror, darkness and incertitude of life founded upon the void is a plague in the "noon of life" (*U,* 394.06, cf. 207.24–26), and is more proper to the obscure periods of "prenativity and postmortemity" (*U,* 394.06–07). He restates the theme that birth is the beginning of death: "And as the ends and ultimates of all things accord in some mean and measure with their inceptions and originals, that same multiplicit concordance which leads forth growth from birth accomplishing by a retrogressive metamorphosis that minishing and ablation towards the final which is agreeable unto nature so is it with our subsolar being" (*U,* 394.08–13). He extends the theme to include Bloom, "Ikey Moses" (*U,* 201.01): "first saved from water of old Nile, among bulrushes, a bed of fasciated wattles" (*U,* 394.15–16).

When Punch Costello calls upon Stephen to sing a song, "*Etienne chanson*" (*U,* 394.24), he replies with a parody of Proverbs 9:1, "wisdom hath built herself a house, this vast majestic longstablished vault, the crystal palace of the Creator all in applepie order, a penny for him who finds the pea" (*U,* 394.25–28). The God of Creation has become for him a cheating confidence man; his world is a "house that Jack built." But God, the "shout in the street" (*U,* 34.33), thunders at Stephen's blasphemy, causing him to wax pale and shrink together. Although he tries to "dye his desperation" (*U,* 395.06) with drink and more boasting, and Bloom explains to him that the thunder is "all of the order of a natural phenomenon" (*U,* 395.15), Stephen cannot drown his fear. As in *A Portrait,* he still imagines "that there is a malevolent reality behind those things I say I fear" (*P,* 243.20–21). He still cannot serve and "make more shows according as men do with wives which Phenomenon has commanded them to do by the book Law" (*U,* 395.31–33). He has lost the holiness of his youth because of "a certain whore of eyepleasing exterior" (*U,* 395.39–40), recalling the prostitute in *A Portrait* who helped Stephen to set his soul "going forth to experience, unfolding itself sin by sin, spreading abroad the balefire of its burning stars and folding back upon itself, fading slowly, quenching its own lights and fires. They were quenched: and the cold darkness filled chaos" (*P,* 103.15–19).

Although Joyce might have found a model for the "whore Bird-in-the-Hand (which was within all foul plagues, monsters and a wicked devil)" (*U,* 396.07–08) in almost any anti-prostitution tract, and did, in fact, rely heavily on Bunyan, an interesting parallel exists in *Aristotle's Master-Piece,* the pseudonymous handbook of sex education, editions of which are found as early as 1694, perused that afternoon by Bloom while looking for an erotic book to bring home to Molly: "Crooked botched print. Plates: infants cuddled in a ball in bloodred wombs like livers of slaughtered cows. Lots of them like that at this moment all over the world. All butting with their skulls to get out of it. Child born every minute somewhere. Mrs. Purefoy" (*U,* 235.19–24). In chapter six of his *Master-Piece,* "Aristotle" contrasts wives with harlots and, in doing so, uses some of the same images found in the "Oxen."

Seeing our blessed Savior and his Apostles detested obscene and unlawful Lusts, and pronounced those to be excluded the Kingdom of Heaven, that polluted themselves with Adultery and Whoring, I cannot conceive any objection be made thereto, or what Face such lewd Persons can have to colour their Impieties; who hating Matrimony, make it their Study how they may live freely and licentiously without Marriage; but certainly, in so doing, they rather seek to themselves Torment, Anxiety and Disquietude, then certain Pleasure, besides the hazard of their Immortal Souls; for certain it is, that Mercenary Love, or as the Wise Man calls them, Harlots Smiles, *cannot be true and sincere; and therefore not pleasant, but rather a Net laid to betray such as trust them, into all Mischief, as* Solomon *observes by the* Young Man, *who turned aside to an Harlot's House,* going, said he, *as a Bird to the Snare of the Fowler, or as an Ox to the Slaughter, till a Dart is struck through the Liver. Nor in this Case can they have Children, those sweet and endearing Pledges of Conjugal Love, or if they have, they will rather redound to their Shame than Comfort; Harlots likewise are like Swallows, Singing and Chattering to their Morning Walk, and Summer Season of Prosperity, but the black stormy Winter of Adversity coming they take Wing, and pass into other Regions, to expand themselves before a warmer Sun; but a vertuous, chast Wife, fixing intire Love upon her Husband, and submitting to him as her Head, and him by whose Direction she ought to steer in all lawful Courses will, like a faithful Companion, share patiently with him in both Adversities, run with chearfulness through all Difficulties and Dangers, though never so hazardous, to preserve or assist him in Poverty, sickness, or whatever else is incident to Humane Frailty, acting according to her Duty in all things, when a proud imperious Harlot, will do no more than she list, even in the prosperous Day and is like a Horse-leach, ever craving, and never satisfied, still seeming displeased if she have not every thing she desires, not regarding the Ruin and Misery of him, she with flattering and feigning Charms pretends to admire, and doat upon him, using to confirm her Hypocrisie, with* Crocodile's *Tears, Vows, and Swoonings, when her Gallant is to depart for a while, or seems to deny her immoderate Desire; but this lasts no longer than she can gratifie her Appetite, and prey upon his Fortunes.* Conradus Gesner *tells us a Story,* That a young Man travelling from *Athens* to *Thebes,* met by the way a Beautiful Lady, as to his Appearance she seemed to be adorned with all Perfections of Beauty, glittering with Gold and Precious Stones, who saluted him, and invited him to her House in an adjacent Village, pretending to be exceedingly enamour'd of him, and declared she had a long time watch'd the opportunity to find him alone, that she might declare the extream Passion she conceived for him. When he came to her House, he found it to appearance very sumptuously built, and gloriously furnish'd with whate'er could seem costly and gay, which so far wrought upon his Covetous Inclination, *that he resolv'd to cut off his intended Journey, and comply with her desire; but whilst she was leading him to see the pleasant Places, came by a* Holy Pilgrim; *who perceiving in what danger the Youth was, resolved to see him in his right Senses, and shew him what he imagined real, was quite otherwise;* so that by powerful Prayer the Mist was taken from before the Youth's Eyes, whenas he beheld his Lady ugly, deformed and monstrous, and that whate'er had appear'd *glorious and beautiful,* was only *Trash.* Then he made her confess *what she was,* and *her design upon the Young Man,* which she did, saying, *She was a* Lamiae *or* Fury, *and that she had enchanted him on purpose to get him unto her Power, that she might devour him.* This Passage may be fitly alluded to Harlots, who draw those that follow their misguided Lights, into Places of Danger and Difficulty, even till they have shipwrecked their Fortunes, and leave them to struggle with the tempestuous Waves of Adversity.[20]

But Stephen and his companions are more intent on immediate sexual gratification than on heeding the word of a pilgrim. Fornication is fun, they say, and a "stout shield of oxengut" (*U,* 396.17) will prevent both venereal disease and conception, so that their sins against fertility, like the childbirths described at the beginning of the chapter, are "from all accident possibility removed" (*U,* 384.13). A condemning voice intrudes, however, warning them that "for their abuses and their spillings" (*U,* 396.25–26), their souls too will be spilled, a possible reminder of Stephen's description of Epictetus in *A Portrait,* "An old gentleman...who said that the soul is very like a bucketful of water" (*P,* 187.22–23). Epictetus also taught a doctrine of self-renunciation, a virtue which neither Stephen nor his comrades can abide in their quest for sexual gratification.

Included in the condemnation are Lynch, Madden, Costello, Lenehan, Dixon, Stephen, and Bloom. For some reason, Crotthers has been omitted from this catalogue. There is no indication that he has left the room since he "sang young Malachi's praise of that beast the unicorn" (*U,* 389.32–33), and he appears later in the chapter to "extol the virile potency of the old bucko that could still knock another child" out of Mina Purefoy (*U,* 408.29–31), to ask Bannon to "pass him a flagon of cordial waters" (*U,* 404.15–16), to advance the "hypothesis of a plasmic memory" (*U,* 411.20–21), and to attribute the vast majority of infant demises "to neglect, private or official, culminating in the exposure of newborn infants, the practice of criminal abortion or in the atrocious crime of infanticide" (*U,* 419.10–13). Perhaps, since he does not seem to take part in the general blasphemy as completely as his companions, affirming in fact Theodore's "virile potency," he is less guilty than they are and less deserving of condemnation.

The scope of narration now moves beyond the confines of the hospital to describe the rain falling on the city. Paddy Dignam is "laid in clay" (*U,* 396.28) and the bargeman whom Bloom saw saluting the coffin (*U,* 99.23–24) and who prompted Father Conmee's meditations on Divine Providence (*U,* 221.34–41) announces that drought is general all over Ireland. People are saying that the "big wind of last February a year" (*U,* 396.38 — February 26–27, 1903) was "a small thing beside this barrenness" (*U,* 396.39). But the rain has come, driving the Dubliners indoors and falling on Buck Mulligan and Alec Bannon, Milly Bloom's boyfriend, as they meet and set out for the hospital.

The company at the hospital is described once again. Crotthers, "a Scots fellow" (*U,* 397.24–25), has reappeared, but Costello is not included this time, an omission for which I can find no explanation. Leopold Bloom is there "for a languor he had but was now better, he having dreamed tonight a strange fancy of his dame Mrs Moll with red slippers on in a pair of Turkey trunks which is thought by those in ken to be for a change" (*U*, 397.26–30). Bloom had remembered this dream, which he actually had the night before, after masturbating on the beach: "Dreamt last night? Wait. Something confused. She had red slippers on. Turkish. Wore the Breeches. Suppose she does" (*U*, 381.11–12). If there is to be a change in Bloom's life, it may begin with Molly getting breakfast for him on the following morning (*U*, 783.01–04). Whether she will reverse their usual practice or not is an unanswerable question, but, corresponding to Bloom's dream, she thinks before she falls asleep, "Id love to have a long talk with an intelligent welleducated person Id have to get a nice pair of red slippers like those Turks with the fez used to sell or yellow" (*U*, 780.01–03), indicating a point of contact between her thoughts and Bloom's.[21]

The Purefoys are then described with all their progeny: " 'Tis her ninth chick to live, I hear, and Lady day bit off her last chick's nails that was then a twelvemonth and with other three all breastfed that died written out in a fair hand in the king's bible" (*U*, 397.36–39).[22] The reason that Mina "bit off her last chick's nails" was evidently to prevent him from becoming a thief, according to Joyce's notes: "Cut nails after 1 year else thief with teeth" (NS, 8.100). But Joyce has not explained on the notesheets why, at this point in the chapter, Mina has had twelve children, nine of whom have survived, and she will later be described as having had nine children, eight of whom have survived (*U*, 421.11–17). As with Costello's absence, I can find no explanation for this discrepancy.

This chatty passage ends with a summary: "In sum an infinite great fall of rain and all refreshed" (*U*, 398.01–02) with some fertility restored to the Irish wasteland, but there are those who warn that "after wind and water fire shall come" (*U*, 398.03–04). These three modes of destruction, common in the Bible, all appear in the "Oxen." The wind of last February a year is followed by the rain of June 16, and, as the drinkers leave the pub at the end of the chapter, they see the fire brigade rushing by, prompting Stephen to announce that "even now that day is at hand when he shall come to judge the world by fire. Pflaap! *Ut implerentur scripturae*" (*U*, 428.10–11).

As we return to the common-room, Lenehan is telling Stephen that the letter about the hoof and mouth disease, given to Stephen by Mr. Deasy that morning, has appeared in the evening paper. The description of Lenehan is essentially the same as that which appeared in Joyce's story, *Two Gallants*:

Most people considered Lenehan a leech, but in spite of this reputation, his adroitness and eloquence had always prevented his friends from forming any general policy against him. He had a brave manner of coming up to a party of them in a bar and of holding himself nimbly at the borders of the company until he was included in a round. He was a sporting vagrant armed with a vast stock of stories, limericks and riddles. He was insensitive to all kinds of discourtesy. No one knew how he achieved the stern task of living, but his name was vaguely associated with racing tissues.[23]

The slaughtering of the animals infected with the hoof and mouth disease is the most overt reference to the slaying of the sacred oxen of Helios Hyperion. The presence of the disease in Ireland connotes also the sickness of Anglo-Irish relations and the moribund state of the Irish populace in general. Bloom and Molly have not escaped the plague; when Molly looks at Bloom sleeping with his head at the foot of the bed she thinks, "its well he doesnt kick or he might knock out all my teeth breathing with his hand on his nose like that Indian god...I suppose he used to sleep at the foot of the bed too with his big square feet up in his wifes mouth" (*U,* 771.33–41).

Talk of Irish bulls and Anglo-Irish relations leads to a discussion of the "Bull of Laudabiliter" sent by Pope Adrian IV (Nicholas Breakspear, an Englishman) to Henry II, granting Ireland to the English king. It modulates into the establishment by another "Lord Harry," Henry VIII, of the Church of England. The basis for the resentment which leads the men of the island to "put to sea to recover the main of America" (*U,* 401.26) is that Ireland is historically the butt of betrayal and oppression, by both her English and Roman masters. The entire "bull" discussion is an amusing variation on the complaint uttered by the Citizen at Barney Kiernan's earlier in the day: "Where are our missing twenty millions of Irish should be here today instead of four, our lost tribes? And our potteries and textiles, the finest in the world!... What do the yellowjohns of Anglia owe us for our ruined trade and our ruined hearths? And the beds of the Barrow and the Shannon they won't deepen with millions of acres of marsh and bog to make us all die of consumption" (*U,* 326.11–14, 29–32).

As Lynch sings his anticlerical song

—*Pope Peter's but a pissabed.*
A man's a man for a' that

(*U,* 401.28–30)

Mulligan and Bannon enter the room. Mulligan hands out cards to those present which state: "*Mr. Malachi Mulligan, Fertiliser and Incubator, Lambay Island*" (*U,* 402.01–02). He explains his intention to establish a human stud farm "to be named *Omphalos* with an obelisk hewn and erected after the fashion of Egypt" (*U,* 402.31–32). Stuart Gilbert describes the *omphalos* theme in *Ulysses* as "at once a symbol of birth...of the strand that links back generation to generation and of a legendary eastern isle embossed on a smooth shield of sea, a lost paradise."[24] It is also, he says, quoting Mme. Blavatsky's *Isis Unveiled,* "'the circle of the sun,' the seat of internal divine light."[25] The phallic symbolism of the "obelisk" is obvious. Mulligan's project, however, is somewhat less mystical, reminding one of Bloom's complaint, "Dirt gets rolled up in your navel" (*U,* 85.07–08), as it does throughout this chapter obscuring the sun and divine light. His project is little more than a plan to establish his own private harem under the guise of ridding society of the evils of sterility. His pledge that "The poorest kitchen-wench no less than the opulent lady of fashion, if so be their constructions, and their tempers were warm persuaders for their petitions, would find in him their man" (*U,* 402.37–40) parodies the charitable intent of the maternity hospital, "whatever care the patient in that all-hardest of woman hour chiefly required and not solely for the copiously opulent but also for her who not being sufficiently moneyed scarcely and often not even scarcely could subsist valiantly and for an inconsiderable emolument was provided" (*U,* 384.13–18). Mulligan's choice of a name for his farm indicates that his plan is an inversion of the principles of the "light one, bright one" who brings "quickening and wombfruit." He is less concerned with promoting fertility than with delivering himself of his spleen of lustihead.

Mulligan notices Bloom at the table and asks if he is "in need of any professional assistance" (*U,* 403.33), to which Bloom replies, "preserving his proper distance" (*U,* 403.34–35), that he has come to inquire about Mrs. Purefoy. His solicitous attitude is in distinct contrast to Mulligan's flippancy and the speed with which the conversation shifts from him points out how misplaced and little regarded he and his feelings are in this gathering. Dixon then asks Mulligan if his sudden exhibition of sexual prowess is caused by the fact that he is himself pregnant. In answer Mulligan declares, "There's a belly that never bore a bastard" (*U,* 404.05–06). Male pregnancy is a theme that occurs often in *Ulysses.* In the library, during the discussion of the "mystical estate" of fatherhood, Stephen says, "Boccaccio's Calandrino was the first and last man who felt himself with child" (*U,* 207.18–20 — The allusion is to the *Decameron,* ninth day, third story, where Calandrino's friends, in order to relieve him of his money, convince him that he is pregnant and charge him exorbitant fees for bogus medicine to rid him of his child). Stephen's talk incites Mulligan's claim, "I am big with child. I have an unborn child in my brain. Pallas Athena! A play! The play's the thing! Let me parturiate!" (*U,* 208.24–26). But Mulligan's progeny resembles the daughter of Milton's Satan more than that of Jove, and is a flagrant violation of the command of "the god Bringforth."

Everyman His own Wife
or
A Honeymoon in the Hand
(a national immorality in three orgasms)
by
Ballocky Mulligan

(*U,* 216.35-40)

Of Mulligan's play one might think, as did Stephen in *A Portrait* of his own thoughts, "His mind bred vermin. His thoughts were lice born of the sweat of sloth" (*P,* 234.11-12).

Bloom, too, parturiates; during one of his hallucinations in Bella Cohen's brothel he gives birth to octuplets, who correspond to the "eight beatitudes" (*U,* 509.09-16) and to the drinkers in the hospital:

> *(Bloom...bears eight male yellow and white children. They appear on a redcarpeted staircase adorned with expensive plants. All are handsome, with valuable metallic faces, wellmade, respectably dressed and wellconducted, speaking five modern languages fluently and interested in various arts and sciences. Each has his name printed in legible letters on his shirtfront: Nasodoro, Goldfinger, Chrysostomos, Maindoree, Silversmile, Silberselber, Vifargent, Panargyros. They are immediately appointed to positions of high public trust in several different countries as managing directors of banks, traffic managers of railways, chairmen of limited liability companies, vice chairmen of hotel syndicates.)*

(*U,* 494.24-36)

Like Mulligan's offspring, Bloom's suit his personality and interests. They are grotesque versions of what he would have liked Rudy to become, "I could have helped him on in life. I could. Make him independent. Learn German too" (*U,* 89.13-14).

Artistic creation, Stephen's version of male childbearing, is more than once described in *A Portrait*. When Stephen is inspired to write his villanelle, "*Are you not weary of ardent ways,*" he thinks, "O! In the virgin womb of the imagination the word was made flesh" (*P,* 217.22-23). Earlier he had told Lynch, "So far as this side of esthetic philosophy [the definition of beauty] extends Aquinas will carry me all along the line. When we come to the phenomena of artistic conception, artistic gestation and artistic reproduction I require a new terminology and a new personal experience" (*P,* 209.32-36). This theme is echoed by Stephen's statement in the "Oxen," "In woman's womb word is made flesh but in the spirit of the maker all flesh that passes becomes the word that shall not pass away. This is the postcreation" (*U,* 391.21-23). Woman brings forth a temporal creature, the artist an eternal one. Thusfar, however, Stephen's genuis has fathered no more than a "capful of light odes" (*U,* 415.10-11), while eight (or nine, or twelve, as the case may be) little Purefoys can call Mina mother.

The announcement of the birth of the latest Purefoy, which happy event probably took place while Mulligan was talking about his "national fertilising farm to be named *Omphalos*" (*U,* 402.31), is made twice (*U,* 406.29, 408.10-11), and is preceded by the ringing of bells, thrice repeated (*U,* 404.09-10; 405.40; 406.01), paralleling the ringing of the bells at the elevation of the host in the Mass and the triple invocations which begin the chapter. The repetition of the announcement and of the bells emphasizes the importance of the birth of the Purefoy child, which is the main event in this chapter and one of the high points of the novel, since this is the only child born in *Ulysses*. At each occurrence the ringing becomes more insistent, as it tries to pierce the alcoholic murkiness of the befuddled minds of the drinkers. It begins as "some larum in the antechamber" (*U,* 404.09-10), becomes a "bell tinkling in the hall" (*U,* 405.40), until finally "a bell rang" (*U,* 406.01) and Miss Callan enters to call Dr. Dixon away to the delivery room.

At the first ringing of the bell the narrative, interrupted "at a salient point" (*U,* 404.13-14), turns back upon itself to the point at which Mulligan asked Bloom if he needed any professional assistance, and Bannon, "The young gentleman, his friend, overjoyed as he was at a passage that had befallen him, could not forbear to tell it his nearest neighbour" (*U,* 403.27-30), Crotthers. The passage that has befallen Bannon is his encounter with Milly Bloom, whose picture he carries in a locket tied about his neck, just as Bloom carries Molly's picture in his wallet (*U,* 418.03-08, 652.23). Milly has evidently captured him as thoroughly as Molly did Leopold, by means of "that sweetest of Thy tyrannies which can hold in thrall the free and the bond, the simple swain and the polished coxcomb, the lover in the heyday of reckless passion and the husband of maturer years" (*U,*405.05-08). Bloom had expected something like this to happen when he read her letter that morning: "Milly too. Young kisses: the first. Far away now past. Mrs. Marion. Reading lying back now, counting the strands of her hair, smiling, braiding. A soft qualm regret, flowed down his backbone, increasing. Will happen, yes. Prevent. Useless: can't move. Girl's sweet light lips. Will happen too. He felt the flowing qualm spread over him. Useless to move now. Lips kissed, kissing kissed. Full gluey woman's lips" (*U,* 67.15-22). The tyranny is indeed a voluptuous one, and in Bloom's contemplation of it he seems to be drawing analogies between Milly's new romance with Bannon, Molly's new romance with Blazes Boylan, and his own attraction to Molly both as "the lover in the heyday of reckless passion and the husband of maturer years." Ironically, Milly's "new coquette cap (a gift for her feast day as she told me)" (*U,* 404.36-37), which so affects Bannon, is the new tam Bloom sent her for her birthday the day before (*U,* 66.03-04). That Bannon threatens to displace Bloom in Milly's affections, just as Boylan is taking his place in Molly's bed, is also indicated by Milly's connection of the two in her letter: "There is a young student comes here some evenings named Bannon his cousins or something are big swells he sings Boylan's (I was on the pop of writing Blazes Boylan's) song about those seaside girls" (*U,* 66.12–15). Bannon voices his regrets that on an outing with Milly he had been unprepared for a sudden rain which overtook them, his comments leading to a discussion of the relative merits of umbrellas and raincoats (which may be read as euphemisms for contraceptive devices). Lynch's Kitty favors an umbrella, he explains, over a cloak and "would dance in a deluge before ever she would starve in such an ark of salvation" (*U,* 405.28–30). She has told him further that there are two things which one should do while naked, "the first is a bath...but at this point a bell tinkling in the hall cut short a discourse which promised so bravely for the enrichment of our store of knowledge" (*U,* 405.39–42).

The bell rings again and Miss Callan enters to inform Dixon that Mrs. Purefoy has had her baby. After she leaves, Costello accuses Dixon of having a romantic attachment with her and claims that she is pregnant. Dixon, suddenly grave and dignified as he assumes his professional role, announces that the baby has been born and rebukes Costello for casting aspersions on Miss Callan's character. His fellows all join in the game, scolding Costello, just as they had earlier when nurse Quigley complained about his "bawdy catch *Staboo Stabella*" (*U,* 392.05) which was also about an illegitimate pregnancy.

The focus now shifts to Bloom and his reaction to Costello's outburst: "he nauseated the wretch that seemed to him a cropeared creature of a misshapen gibbosity born out of wedlock and thrust like a crookback teethed and feet first into the world" (*U,* 407.25–28). Bloom has no respect for "those who create themselves wits at the cost of feminine delicacy" (*U,* 407.39–40). When he complains to his neighbor that "one must have a cold constitution and a frigid genius not to be rejoiced by this freshest news of the fruition of her confinement since she had been in such pain through no fault of hers" (*U,* 408.17–20), the answer, "it was her husband's that put her in that expectation or at least ought to be" (*U,* 408.21–22) recalls the Citizen's question, "And who does he suspect?" (*U,* 338.14), when the fact that Bloom has fathered two children was brought up at Barney Kiernan's. As the students talk, Bloom thinks about "the wonderfully unequal faculty of metempsychosis possessed by them" (*U,* 408.36–37), that the reception of an academic degree should transform these revelers into responsible and respected medical practitioners. Bloom's malapropism, "metempsychosis" for "metamorphosis," may be an allusion to the parodic technique of this chapter, metamorphosis of language showing the successive reincarnations of the artistic Logos.

An intrusive voice now questions Bloom's right to criticize the students and exposes his hypocrisy: "is it that from being a deluder of others he has become at last his own dupe as he is, if report belie him not, his own and only enjoyer?" (*U*, 409.14–16). He has just come in from the beach where, excited by Gerty Macdowell's exhibition, he sinned against fertility by masturbating; his sexual life with Molly has been unfruitful for the past ten years; he "did not scruple, oblivious of the ties of nature, to attempt illicit intercourse with a female domestic drawn from the lowest strata of society" (*U*, 409.24–27 — Mary Driscoll, the servant, returns to haunt Bloom in a hallucination as he is on his way to Bella Cohen's brothel [*U*, 460–61], and is recalled by Molly in her soliloquy [*U*, 739.23–740.06]). "It ill becomes him to preach that gospel" (*U*, 409.32–33).

After Bloom is sufficiently chastised and exposed, the narrative turns back once again to the announcement of the birth. As soon as Dixon leaves, the assembled company breaks out "into a strife of tongues" (*U*, 410.18–19), discussing all manner of obstetrical oddities, "in a word all the cases of human nativity which Aristotle has classified in his masterpiece with chromolithographic illustrations" (*U*, 411.05–07). The allusion is to *Aristotle's Master-Piece,* chapter five of which is entitled "*Of Monsters, and monstrous Births, and the reasons thereof, according to the Opinion of sundry Learned Men, with serious Considerations, whether Monsters are endued with reasonable Souls.*"[26] Although chapter five does not contain all the cases of human nativity referred to in this passage, examples of abnormal birth abound throughout "Aristotle's" work. In chapter three he discusses the role of imagination in determining the appearance of the child and explains why "The wise father knows his own child" (*U*, 413.25–27):

> In case of the Similitude, nothing is more powerful than the Imagination of the Mother, for if she conceive in her Mind, or do by Chance fasten her Eyes upon any Object, and imprint it in her memory, the Child in its *outward parts* frequently has some representation thereof; so whilst a Man or Woman are in the Act of Copulation, if the Woman earnestly behold his Countenance, and fix her Mind thereon; without all peradventure, the Child will resemble the Father; nay, so powerful is its operation, that tho' a Woman be in unlawful Copulation, yet if Fear, or any thing else causes her to fix her Mind upon her Husband, the Child will resemble him, tho' he never got it. The same effect, according to the *Opinion* of the Learned, Proceeds from Imagination in cause of Warts, Mold-spots, Stains, Dashes, and the Figures of strange things, tho' indeed they sometimes happen thro' Frights or extravagant Longings: Many Women there are that seeing a Hare cross them, when great with Child, will through the strength of *Imagination,* bring forth a Child with a hairy Lip. Some Children again are born with flat Noses, wry Mouths, great blubber lips, and ill-shap'd Bodies, and most ascribe the reason to the strange conceit of the *Mother,* who has busied her Eyes and Mind upon some ill-shaped or distorted Creatures; Therefore it properly behoves all Women with Child to avoid any monstrous Sight, or at least to have a steadfast Mind not easily fixed upon any thing more than another.[27]

The abnormalities listed by "Aristotle" are similar to the "harelip, breast-mole, supernumerary digits, Negro's inkle, strawberry mark and portwine stain" (*U,,* 411.16–17) in the "Oxen," but the primary significance of the reference here to "Aristotle" is that it indicates the unscientific, popularized level at which the conversation is being conducted. An "outlandish dele-gate" supports the "theory of copulation between women and the males of brutes, his authority being his own avouchment in support of fables such as that of the Minotaur which the genius of the elegant Latin poet has handed down to us in the pages of his Metamorphoses" (*U,* 411.24–30), recalling Stephen's list of "incests and bestialities," mentioned in the library, which included, "Sons with mothers, sires with daughters, lesbic sisters, loves that dare not speak their name, nephews with grandmothers, jailbirds with keyholes, queens with prize bulls" (*U,* 207.36–41). In the brothel Ste-phen says, "Queens lay with prize bulls. Remember Pasiphae for whose lust my grandoldgrossfather made the first confessionbox" (*U,* 569.08–10), a reference to his Dedalean ancestry. The tale of the Minotaur comple-ments to some extent that of the Homeric "Oxen of the Sun." Minos II, for whom Daedalus built the labyrinth to house the Minotaur, was a descendant of Minos I, the legendary first king of Crete and son of Europa by Jove, who took the form of a bull in order to abduct her. Unlike the companions of Odysseus, who offended Helios by sacrificing sacred cattle, Minos II offended Neptune by refusing to sacrifice a bull which the god had sent to him for that purpose. As punishment for his crime, Neptune caused Pasi-phae, wife of Minos, to copulate with the bull and conceive a monster, the Minotaur. To protect the citizens of Crete from the ravages of the monster, Daedalus constructed a maze, to which were brought each nine years, seven young men and seven virgins as food for the Minotaur. This practice continued until Theseus, aided by Ariadne, daughter of Minos and Pas-iphae, killed the monster.[28] The parallel is a loose one, involving, besides the plentitude of bulls in both stories, the offense against a god and the senseless sacrifice attendant upon the crime.

Mulligan now takes the floor, "postulating as the supremest object of desire a nice clean old man" (*U,* 411.34–35), but before he can develop his idea, a "juridical and theological dilemma in the event of one Siamese twin predeceasing the other" (*U,* 411.37–39) is resolved by Stephen's citation of "the ecclesiastical ordinance forbidding man to put asunder what God has joined" (*U,* 412.03–04). As Mulligan continues his tale, Haines comes in and tells Mulligan to meet him "at Westland row station at ten past eleven" (*U,* 412.26). His appearance is accompanied by a cluster of verbal echoes, primarily from Haines' nightmare about the black panther (*U,* 4.23–30), Stephen's ghost story version of *Hamlet* (*U,* 187.39 ff.), and the murder of Samuel Childs (*U,* 100.01–17, 139.21–35). This elaborate texture should not obscure the fact that, if it is to be consistent with the rest of the narrative, this passage is an elaboration of Malachi's postulation of a "nice clean old man" as the supremest object of desire. As Stephen and Mulligan stood on the steps of the library earlier in the day, Bloom passed between them: "A dark back went before them. Step of a pard, down, out by the gateway, under portcullis barbs" (*U,* 218.01-02). Mulligan describes him as "The wandering jew.... Did you see his eye? He looked upon you to lust after you. I fear thee, ancient mariner. O, Kinch, thou art in peril. Get thee a breechpad" (*U,* 217.35-38). Bloom, dressed, like Stephen, in mourning, is a black pard, the panther who haunts Haines' dreams. He is old, a wandering Jew; as Ulysses he is an old seaman, an ancient mariner. Mulligan warns against the meeting of Stephen and Bloom just as Mr. Deasy had warned him against the Jews that morning (*U,* 33.28 ff.). That "The black panther was himself the ghost of his own father" (*U,* 412.33-34) connects Bloom with Hamlet *père* (*U,* 18.11-17) and Stephen with Hamlet *fils* "striving to be atoned with the Father" (*U,* 18.37-38). Although the verbal echoes concerning the Childs murder case are taken from Bloom's thoughts as he passes the deserted Childs home on the way to Paddy Dignam's funeral, the murders of Samuel Childs and the elder Hamlet were connected by Stephen in the newspaper office on the basis that both men were killed in their sleep by their brothers and both, like Bloom, were cuckolded (*U,* 139.26-27). The black panther that Haines fears and the old man that Mulligan warns against, yet postulates as the supremest object of desire, is the elder Hamlet with which Stephen must be atoned. That the influence of Haines and Mulligan will disappear and be replaced by Bloom's is foreshadowed by Haines' request that Mulligan meet him at Westland row station; it is there that they will desert Stephen, and that Bloom will finally decide to follow him on the train to nighttown: "Wildgoose chase this. Disorderly houses. Lord knows where they are gone. Drunks cover distance double quick. Nice mixup. Scene at Westland row.... What am I following him for? Still, he's the best of that lot. If I hadn't heard about Mrs Beaufoy Purefoy I wouldn't have gone and wouldn't have met. Kismet. He'll lose that cash." (*U,* 452.05-13, cf. *U,* 620.10-16.)

As if to convince himself that he is not really an old man, Bloom's thoughts return to his schooldays (*U,* 413.04-10) and to his early days as a traveling salesman (*U,* 413.10-23). But with thoughts of his own father comes the realization that "he himself is paternal and these about him might be his sons. Who can say? The wise father knows his own child" (*U,* 413.25-27), recalling Simon Dedalus' quip, "the wise child that knows her own father" (*U,* 88.19-20), which was repeated by Bloom in the Ormond Bar with the question "Me?" (*U,* 273.08). Bloom remembers his first sexual experience with Bridie Kelly, when he might have fathered a child, but the narrator reveals that this was not to be so, "No son of thy loins is by thee. There is none now to be for Leopold, what Leopold was for Rudolph" (*U,* 413.42–414.02).

As Bloom's reverie deepens, the voices of those around him fade away and a vision rises up before him of "a mare leading her fillyfoal" (*U,* 414.09), Molly and Milly, his wife and daughter from whom he is growing farther apart. They fade away; Agendath Netaim, his potential eastern paradise, is "a waste land, a home of screechowls and the sandblind upupa" (*U,* 414.13). Instead, he now sees an "Ominous, revengeful, zodiacal host!" (*U,* 414.20) tramping onward to drink the salt waters of the dead sea. The "murderers of the sun" (*U,* 414.24) pass and "the equine portent grows again" (*U,* 414.27); Bloom's daughter Milly blends with Martha Clifford, the object of his epistolary romance, and with Gerty MacDowell, the seaside girl whose skin, like Molly's is covered by a "fine veil or web they have all over the skin, fine like what do you call it gossamer" (*U,* 374.40–41). Her gossamer veil winds and coils, "writhing in the skies a mysterious writing till after a myriad metamorphoses of symbol, it blazes, Alpha, a ruby and triangled sign upon the forehead of Taurus" (*U,* 414.38–41), portending a new beginning. The entire passage recalls Bloom's first reading of the Agendath Netaim advertisement that morning on a piece of old newspaper used to wrap sales in Dlugacz's butcher shop. He pictures the lush tropical gardens of the Near East and of "Spain, Gibraltar, Mediterranean, the Levant" (*U,* 60.40–41). As a cloud passes over the sun, he realizes that the Near East is also a land of deserts, of the dead sea; "It bore the oldest, the first race....the oldest people. Wandered far away over all the earth, captivity to captivity, multiplying, dying being born everywhere. It lay there now. Now it could bear no more. Dead: an old woman's: the grey sunken cunt of the world" (*U,* 61.14–19). As he hurries home to Molly, "Quick warm sunlight came running from Berkeley Road, swiftly, in slim sandals, along the brightening footpath. Runs, she runs to meet me, a girl with gold hair on the wind" (*U,* 61.32–34). The pattern of images is the same in both instances: ripeness and productivity followed by the realization of desolation and sterility which gives way to a rebirth and youth. Bloom sees the "cycles of cycles of generation that have lived" (*U,* 414.05), the eternal round of birth and death, the supplantation of the old by the young. His vision occurs while he is staring at the red triangular label on a bottle of Bass number one ale, a symbol not only of Trinacria, but also of the vagina, entrance to the womb and promise of continuance of the race as well. It may also remind him of the "redlabelled bottle" of poison with which his father committed suicide (*U,* 97.02), in which case the bottle of Bass would function as an image of both life and death, womb and tomb; the ale quickening the conversation while deadening the intellect, provoking sexual desire, but taking away the performance. That the "murderers of the sun" are zodiacal indicates that they are the constellations which kill the sun, driving it below the western horizon and are in turn driven away by the rebirth of the "daystar" in the new dawn, suggesting that although Bloom's son Rudy has died, a new son, Stephen, will rise to replace him.[29]

While Bloom is lost in thought, Costello, evidently a schoolfellow of Stephen's at Clongowes Wood college "in Conmee's time" (*U,* 415.01), asks Stephen what has become of their childhood friends, "Glaucon, Alcibiades, Pisistratus" (*U,* 415.02). Neither Stephen nor Costello has followed their careers, but Stephen boasts that he can recreate them by his art: "You have spoken of the past and its phantoms, Stephen said. Why think of them? If I call them into life across the waters of Lethe will not the poor ghosts troop to my call? Who supposes it. I, Bous Stephanomenous, bullock, befriending bard, am lord and giver of their live" (*U,* 415.03–07). Stephen assumes for a moment the role of Ulysses, calling the ghosts from Hades, including that of his mother, in Book XI of the *Odyssey.* He is also the Holy Spirit, the "Lord and Giver of life" in the Nicene Creed, transmuting "all flesh that passes" into the "word that shall not pass away" (*U,* 391.22–23). "Bullockbefriending bard" is the name Stephen foresaw Mulligan giving him that morning when he agreed to help place Mr. Deasy's article on the hoof and mouth disease (*U,* 36.02–03), which Lenehan tried unsuccessfully to find in the evening paper earlier in the chapter (*U,* 398.10–15). Publication of this letter was Stephen's one literary success of the day, a meager output for the Holy Spirit incarnate. Joyce may also have had in mind his own article, "Politics and Cattle Disease," which appeared in the *Freeman's Journal* for September 10, 1912. In it he praises and defends the Irish farmers for their honesty and vigilance in dealing with the epidemic of hoof and mouth disease and condemns the unfair treatment they have received at the hands of the vested interests in the British parliament.[30]

Lynch reminds Stephen that thusfar only "a capful of light odes can call your genius father" (*U,* 415.10–11), but expresses the hope that Stephen will go on to produce more substantial works. "Have no fear," Lenehan assures Lynch, "He could not leave his mother an orphan" (*U,* 415.15). Without his bidding it, the ghosts of his past and the sterility of his present way of life rise up to confront him. In the brothel, his mother will reappear to tell him, "I pray for you in my other world. Get Dilly to make you that boiled rice every night after your brain work. Years and years I loved you, O my son, my firstborn, when you lay in my womb" (*U,* 581.16–18 – cf. "Before born babe bliss had. Within womb won he worship," *U,* 384.32). Stephen has fulfilled neither his own ambitions nor his mother's hopes for him. Rather than spending his nights at "brain work," he "murders his goods with whores" and drunkards. He is serving neither the church of his mother nor the light of artistic creation.

The talk now turns to the Ascot Gold Cup race, on which both Madden and Lenehan have lost money. Sceptre, the favorite who lost the race, "is not the filly that she was," says Lenehan. "By gad, sir, a queen of them. Do you remember her, Vincent?" (*U*, 415.36-37). Lynch answers with a description of his own queen, Kitty, with whom he had almost been surprised that afternoon by Father Conmee (*U*, 416.10-14, 224.25-32). "But he had been kind," Lynch says. "In going by he had blessed us" (*U*, 416.18-19). When Lenehan, to drown his sorrows over his loss, reaches for the bottle of ale at which Bloom had been staring, Mulligan stops him: "His soul is far away. It is as painful perhaps to be awakened from a vision as to be born. Any object intensely regarded, may be a gate of access to the incorruptible eon of the gods. Do you not think it, Stephen?" (*U*, 416.24-27). Stephen agrees, in Theosophical language which seems to relate to Bloom's vision, and which contains some of the same expressions found in the earlier parody of the Theosophists in "Cyclops" (*U*, 301.13-302.11).

The narrator, who evidently has no patience with "the preposterous surmise about him being in some description of a doldrums or other or mesmerised" (*U*, 416.35-37), explains that Bloom is simply "recollecting two or three private transactions of his own which the other two were as mutually innocent of as the babe unborn" (*U*, 417.11-13). Bloom snaps out of his trance, sees that Lenehan wants a drink, and pours it for him. The drinkers, for the fourth time in the chapter, are named and described: Crotthers, Lynch, Costello, Madden, Dixon, who is upstairs attending Mrs. Purefoy, Bannon, Mulligan, Stephen, Lenehan, and "that vigilant wanderer, soiled by the dust of travel and combat and stained by the mire of an indelible dishonour, but from whose steadfast and constant heart no lure or peril or threat of degradation could ever efface the image of that voluptuous loveliness which the inspired pencil of Lafayette has limned for ages yet to come" (*U*, 418.03-08), Leopold Bloom. This account of Bloom, which complements the earlier condemnation of his hypocrisy (*U*, 409.04-410.06), gives a short resume of his day's activities: wandering the streets of Dublin, fighting with the Citizen in Barney Kiernan's, masturbating on the beach, but ever faithful to Molly. The "image of the voluptuousness" limned by Lafayette, a Dublin photographer, is the same picture he will show Stephen in the cabman's shelter (*U*, 652.23 ff.).

The narrator becomes even more matter of fact, deploring Stephen's addiction to a "perverted transcendentalism. . . . Science, it cannot be too often repeated, deals with tangible phenomena" (*U*, 418.10, .13-14), recalling Bloom's attempt to calm Stephen's fears by explaining that the clap of thunder which had frightened him earlier in the chapter was "all of the order of a natural phenomenon" (*U*, 395.15), and the complaint of the unnamed narrator of the "Cyclops" episode about Bloom: "And then he starts with his jawbreakers about phenomenon and science and this phenomenon and the other phenomenon" (*U*, 304.37–38). The discussion which follows, about "the future determination of sex" (*U*, 418.19) and "infant mortality" (*U*, 418.30–31) is prompted by questions from Bloom, who is always eager to learn more "mixed up things especially about the body and the insides" (*U*, 743.04–05). Although the language appears to be scientific and the embryologists cited are actual authorities, the theories about the determination of sex are not very different from those in *Aristotle's Master-Piece:*

> The act of *Coition* being over, (*wherein the force of Imagination is certainly very prevalent in the causing of the Child to be of this or that Sex*) the Woman (say the *Antients*) must gently repose on her Right Side, with her Head lying low, and her Body sinking down, that by sleeping in that posture, the *Cell* on the Right Side of the *Matrix* may prove the *Place of Conception,* in which is the greatest force of Generative Heat, which is the chief Inducement to the Procreation of *Male* Children, and rarely fails to answer the expectation of those that experience it, especially if they keep themselves warm, and without much Motion, leaning for the most part toward the Right, and drinking a little of *Spirit of Saffron,* and *Juice of Hysop* in a *Glass of Mallaga,* or *Aligant,* when they lie down and rise for the space of a Week. Now the fittest time (they say) for the Procreation of *Male* Children, is when the *Sun* is in *Leo,* and the *Moon's* in *Virgo, Scorpio,* or *Sagittarius.*
>
> This Order they also have observed for a *Female Child,* by lying as aforesaid on the left side, and strongly fancying a *Female* in the time of Procreation, especially if the *Woman* drink the *Decoction* of *Female Mercury,* four days from the first day of Purgation; the *Male Mercury* (both Herbs so called) having the like Operation in the case of a *Male Child;* for the Juice or Decoction of those Simples are of Force, the One to purge the *Right,* and the *other* the *Left Side* of the *Womb,* & thereby open the *Receptacles,* making way for the Seminary of Generation: And the best time to *copulate* for this Sex is, when the Moon is in the *wane,* and the sign in *Libra* or *Aquarius,* for then they will be of a most gentle, affable temper, very fair, and perfect in all their members. *Avicenna,* an Author of good repute, describes the time of *Procreation* thus: *When* (saith he) *the Menses are spent, and the Womb is cleansed, which is commonly five days, or seven at most, if a man lie with his Wife from the first day she is purged to the fifth, she will conceive a Male; but from the fifth to the eighth a Female, and from the eighth to the twelfth a Male again: But after that number of days, perhaps neither distinctly, but both in an* Hermophradite.[31]

The language of the "Oxen" is more impressive, but the quality of the knowledge expressed is little above the level of "Aristotle." Mulligan's plan to restore the "calibre of the race" (*U*, 418.41–42) recalls the "aspect of all very distracting spectacles in various latitudes by our terrestrial orb offered together with images, divine and human, the cogitation of which by sejunct females is to tumescence conducive" (*U*, 384.38–41) from the introduction to this chapter, and is a corollary of "Aristotle's" warning to "avoid any monstrous Sight" while carrying a child.

Lynch proposes the deterministic theory of evolution that all natural occurrences, all births and deaths whether of human beings, flowers or stars, are "subject to a law of numeration as yet unascertained" (*U*, 419.26–27) and, "though productive of pain to some of our feelings (notably the maternal), is nevertheless, some of us think, in the long run beneficial to the race in general in securing thereby the survival of the fittest" (*U*, 419.39–42). The same attitude provided Bloom small consolation earlier in the day when a child's funeral passing by reminded him of Rudy's death: "A dwarf's face mauve and wrinkled like little Rudy's was. Dwarf's body, weak as putty, in a whitelined deal box. Burial friendly society pays. Penny a week for a sod of turf. Our. Little. Beggar. Baby. Meant nothing. Mistake of nature. If it's healthy it's from the mother. If not the man. Better luck next time" (*U*, 96.04–09). Bloom connects Rudy's death with his father's suicide: "That afternoon of the inquest. The redlabelled bottle on the table. The room in the hotel with hunting pictures. . . . Thought he was asleep first. Then saw like yellow streaks on his face. Had slipped down to the foot of the bed. Verdict: overdose. Death by misadventure" (*U*, 97.02–03, .05–08). Unlike the young medical students, Bloom, who has lost both father and son, cannot rationalize away his grief with scientific theories. It is this same unscientific humaneness and compassion that bring him to the hospital and that cause him to grieve for Stephen (*U*, 390.42–391.02) and to follow and protect him.

Stephen's recent loss of his mother adds a note of bitterness to his remark, an example of his "perverted transcendentalism" (*U*, 418.10), that an omnivorous God, a "Ghoul! Chewer of corpses!" (*U*, 10.25, cf. 581.14, .27), who dines regularly on the dregs of humanity, "might possibly find gastric relief in an innocent collation of staggering bob" (*U*, 420.06–08). When he speaks lightly of conception and childbirth, "once a woman has let the cat into the bag. . .she must let it out again or give it life. . .to save her own" (*U*, 420.22–26), Bloom, who cannot easily dismiss the dangers of childbearing, rebukes him quietly, "At the risk of her own" (*U*, 420.26). Stephen's raillery, like his drinking, is an attempt to "dye his desperation," to blot out and overcome the ghosts of his past.

By way of contrast, the narrative focus shifts to Mina Purefoy, "as she reclines there with the motherlight in her eyes, that longing hunger for baby fingers (a pretty sight it is to see), in the first bloom of her new motherhood, breathing a silent prayer of thanksgiving to One above, the Universal Husband" (*U*, 420.37–41). Old Nobodaddy (*U*, 395.04) has become a Universal Husband; instead of an omnivorous being devouring mankind, Mina is hungering for the touch of her child's fingers. If "The sentimentalist is he who would enjoy without incurring the immense debtorship for a thing done" (*U*, 412.29–31, 199.21–22),[32] as Stephen wrote in his telegram to Mulligan, it is the drinkers and fornicators below who are sentimental and Mina and Doady who are the hardheaded realists. The ideals they embody, and which Bloom, despite his failings, approximates, are those extolled as virtues in this chapter, fecundity and a loving family, "the fruit of their lawful embraces" (*U*, 421.02). Mina and Doady have both "fought the good fight" (*U*, 420.34, 421.26). "Well done," says the narrator, "thou good and faithful servant!" (*U*, 421.27–28).

Downstairs from this happy scene Bloom is about to be confronted once more with a vision, "shrouded in the piteous vesture of the past, silent, remote, reproachful" (*U*, 421.41–42). Bloom recalls the first time he met Stephen, seventeen years before, at a party in Roundtown (cf. *U*, 680.06–09). Molly, not yet Bloom's wife, was there, as was Stephen's mother. In Bloom's imagination, Stephen is once again the "lad of four or five in linsey-woolsey" (*U*, 422.19–20). He has changed through the years, but he still "frowns a little...with a perhaps too conscious enjoyment of danger but must needs glance at whiles towards where his mother watches ...with a faint shadow of remoteness or of reproach...in her glad look" (*U*, 422.23–28). Stephen has since lost his mother, just as Bloom had lost his father scarcely a year before the party (*U*, 684.33–35). The fact that Simon Dedalus, Stephen's natural father, is absent from the scene suggests that Bloom is playing the role of father opposite both Molly, his wife-to-be who did not give him a son, and May Dedalus, the mother of Stephen. His empathy for Stephen's loss and his own desire for a son combine to help him decide to follow Stephen, to watch over him as he would his own son.

The narrative continues with an ironically idealized description of the students, comparing them to the shepherds and angels "about a crib in Bethlehem of Juda long ago" (*U*, 422.33–34). The Nativity scene gives way to the drought described earlier (*U*, 396.28–39) and to clouds, "swollen masses turgidly distended" (*U*, 422.36), pregnant with life giving rain, "till in an instant a flash rives their centres and with the reverberation of the thunder the cloudburst pours its torrent, so and not otherwise was the transformation, violent and instantaneous, upon the utterance of the Word" (*U*, 422.39–42). The Word is "Burke's!" (*U*, 423.01), the name of a local pub to which Stephen leads the drinkers. On their way out they meet Dixon, who joins them "with news of placentation ended" (*U*, 423.08). Bloom pauses for a moment to "send a kind word to happy mother and nurseling" (*U*, 423.13–14), and is also off.

The narrator steps forward to praise Theodore Purefoy, "the remarkablest progenitor barring none in this chaffering allincluding most farraginous chronicle" (*U*, 423.25–26). Work, he says, "Toil on, labour like a very bandog and let scholarment and all Malthusiasts go hang" (*U*, 423.29–30). Be guided by faith in the future rather than by the prophets of doom and starvation. Follow the sun god of light and fertility rather than the ways of darkness of sterility. He clearly states Joyce's theme, the parallel between contraception and the slaughter of the sacred oxen, when he says, "Copulation without population! No, say I! Herod's slaughter of the innocents were the truer name" (*U*, 423.38–40). "*Deine Kuh Trubsal melkest Du. Nun trinkst Du die susse Milch des Euters*" (*U*, 424.08–09); "You are milking your cow, Adversity. Now you are drinking the sweet milk of her udders"; you have labored, now reap the fruit of your labor. Echoing the opening words of Horace's "Victory" ode, he says, "*Per deam Partulam et Pertundam nunc est bibendum!*" *(U*, 424.17–18); "By Partula, goddess of childbirth, and Pertunda, goddess of copulation, now must we drink." The entire eulogy is an exuberant restatement of "that evangel simultaneously command and promise which on all mortals with prophecy of abundance or with diminution's menace that exalted of reiteratedly procreating function ever irrevocably enjoined" (*U*, 383.35–39).

If this last passage was full of intoxication and euphoria, celebrating the consummation of a job well done, the rest of the chapter is marked by the drunkenness of the "guzzlingden" (*U*, 424.13), or as Gilbert suggests, "the gift of tongues."[33] The rioters are "All off for a buster, armstrong, hollering down the street" (*U*, 424.19). It is evidently still raining outside, since someone asks "Any brollies or gumboots in the fambly?" (*U*, 424.21–22). Dixon, the "sawbones" (*U*, 424.22), catches up with the group and is followed by Bloom (*U*, 424.27–29). One of the Denzille lane boys (beggars), mistaking Stephen's black hat and mourning clothes for the garb of a clergyman, calls out, "Jay, look at the drunken minister coming out of the maternity hospital" (*U*, 424.24–25), to which Stephen replies by reciting the last blessing from the Mass: "*Benedicat vos omnipotens Deus, Pater et Filius*" (*U*, 424.25–26).[34]

The badinage continues as they "Halt! Heave to" (*U*, 425.04), and enter the pub. When Bloom orders a "Ginger cordial," he is ridiculed: "Chase me, the cabby's caudle" (*U*, 425.09–10), but he is following, intentionally or not, the prescription of "Aristotle" for post-partum mothers: "Present sleep is not convenient, but about four hours after Delivery, she may take Broath, Caudle or what other liquid matter is nourishing, and afterwards if she be disposed to sleep, it may be safely permitted: And this is as much in case of a Natural Birth, as ought immediately to be done."[35] Bloom sets his watch, which stopped at the same time that Molly committed adultery with Boylan (*U*, 425.13–14, cf. 373.39–42), perhaps indicating a new start with time beginning again, and Lenehan describes Molly for Dixon, "Got a prime pair of mincepies, no kid" (*U*, 425.21–22, cf. 234.31–32).

Stephen is saddled with the bill for the drinks, since someone "Seed near free poun on un a spell ago a said war hisn" (*U*, 426.06–07, cf. 391.13–17). Lenehan notices Bantam Lyons, who misinterpreted Bloom's statement that morning that he was going to throw his paper away as a tip to bet on Throwaway in the Ascot Gold Cup race (*U*, 85.42), but was convinced by Lenehan to bet on Sceptre instead (*U*, 335.16–19). Lenehan shifts the blame for the bad tip to someone named Stephen Hand, who steamed open a telegram from "big bug Bass," the owner of Sceptre, which stated "Mare on form hot order" (*U*, 426.23–25).[36] Stephen pays for another round of drinks (*U*, 426.38–42) and notices that Mulligan and Bannon have disappeared to meet Haines; "Where's the buck and Namby Amby?" (*U*, 427.07), he asks. Stephen has been checkmated; he cannot return to his tower. "Kind Kristyann," he asks, "will yu help, yung man hoose frend tuk bungalo kee to find plais whear to lay crown off his hed 2 night" (*U*, 427.09–11).

"Walking Mackintosh of lonely canyon" (*U*, 427.24–25), whom Bloom saw that morning at Paddy Dignam's funeral (*U*, 109.29–110.13), reappears as the drinkers leave the tavern at closing time (*U*, 427.35–38). Someone vomits, someone sings, "Yooka. Night. Mona my thrue love. Yook. Mona, my own love. Ook" (*U*, 427.41–42). The fire brigade passes by, "Pflaap! Pflaap!" (*U*, 428.01), and Stephen invites Lynch to accompany him to nighttown with a parody of Dante Gabriel Rossetti's "The Blessed Damozel" (11.103–04): "We two, she said, will seek the kips where shady Mary is" (*U*, 428.06–07). Lynch notices Bloom following them and asks, "who the sooty hell's the johnny in the black duds?" (*U*, 428.08–09). "Hush!" Stephen answers, "Sinned against the light and even now that day is at hand when he shall come to judge the world by fire" (*U*, 428.09–11). Mr. Deasy had warned Stephen about the Jews who "sinned against the light" (*U*, 34.03), and Stephen's answer, "Who has not?" (*U*, 34.17), has been illustrated in detail by the events of this episode.

The chapter ends as it began, in chaos; but just as the initial chaos cleared into a readable narrative, this final confusion contains hints of regeneration. Lynch sees a picture poster of an "excrement yellow gospeller on the Merrion Hall" (*U*, 428.13–14), and Stephen reads "Elijah is coming washed in the Blood of the Lamb" (*U*, 428.14–15). "Ben Bloom Elijah" (*U*, 345.29) is indeed coming with his gospel of continuity and of perpetual regeneration: "One born every second somewhere. Other dying every second. Since I fed the birds five minutes. Three hundred kicked the bucket. Other three hundred born, washing the blood off, all are washed in the blood of the lamb, bawling Maaaaaa" (*U*, 164.20–25). Whatever Stephen learns from Bloom, it is not the doctrine of personal self-assertion; "No one is anything" (*U*, 164.37), says Bloom. Instead of pride and riotous living, Stephen must learn patience and dedication to his lifetask. Until now he has been one of those "that will and would and wait and never do" (*U,* 424.05–06). Stephen must find his America, "Father Son and Holy Ghost and Jakes M'Carthy" (*U,* 135.23–24), in Leopold, Molly, and "dear dirty Dublin" itself, and "charge to cover like the transpontine bison" (*U,* 424.07).

3

Embryological Framework

Ever since Joyce announced to Frank Budgen that the structure of the "Oxen of the Sun" was linked to the "natural stages of development in the embryo," readers of this chapter have attempted to find some relationship between the text and the nine months of human gestation. Budgen, in his book on the making of *Ulysses*, merely alludes to the fact that embryological correspondences do exist: "The chaste, faithful nurse is the ovum, Bloom, the vital principle, is the spermatozoon. Stephen, the growing and expanding soul, is the embryo, and all are contained within the womb for which the maternity hospital of Dr. Horne is symbol."[1] Stuart Gilbert is only slightly more ambitious:

> Readers of this episode who have some acquaintance with embryology will find many allusions which mark the changes of the embryo, month by month, as it grows to perfection in the womb. Thus, in the first month, it is wormlike, a 'punctus', in the second it has a (relatively) big head, webbed fingers, is eyeless, mouthless, sexless. The mention of fishes 'withouten head' in 'oily water' is a reference to the first month: the vermiform shape and the amniac fluid. Later, Stephen tells how 'at the end of the second month' a human soul is infused and, soon after, we see Mr. Bloom 'lay hand to jaw'; the formation of the jawbone is a feature of the third month. At that stage the embryo has a distinct tail—hence the mutation of 'Oxford' into 'Oxtail'. The reference to 'visual organs commencing to exhibit signs of animation' marks the seventh month. There are many more such correspondences to be detected by the reader of *Ulysses* who, unlike the writer of this study, has more than a superficial acquaintance with the facts of prenatal development.[2]

The characteristics of embryonic development listed by Gilbert agree, with one exception, with those on the gestation chart in the British Museum notesheets. There is no reference on the chart, or anywhere else in the notesheets, to "visual organs commencing to exhibit signs of animation" as a characteristic of fetal growth. It is of course possible that Joyce intended such a correspondence without noting it on these sheets, and, although it does not agree with my own divisions of the chapter, Gilbert is probably correct in calling this a characteristic of the seventh month. If he is, and I have no reason to doubt his word, this would not be the only contrary embryological indication in this chapter. For example, during the first month, according to Gilbert, the embryo is mouthless. Yet prior to "the end of the second month" there occurs a reference to "vampires mouth to mouth" (*U,* 390.03).

Gilbert quotes Stephen's statement that "at the end of the second month a soul was infused" and follows it with an excerpt from *Venus Magique,* according to which the fetus does not receive the breath of life until the seventh month and it is not until the ninth month that "*l'esprit entre dans sa nouvelle residence elementaire; il y connait par une profonde contemplation le Mot indestructible.*"[3] To further confuse the issue, Joyce has written on the notesheets "soul born: conception" (*NS,* 8.123), so that the reader can feel confident that whether he prefers to find the infusion of the soul in the first month, "to have his dear soul in his undeathliness" (*U,* 386.01-02), "at the end of the second month" (*U,* 390.08), or "upon the utterance of the Word" (*U,* 422.42), he is not far from wrong. That there are three infusions may, of course, reflect the three souls postulated by Thomas Aquinas: vegetative, animal, and intellectual.

Gilbert and the gestation chart also agree that "the formation of the jawbone is a feature of the third month." On the notesheets, however, the "lower jaw" appears as a characteristic of the second month (*NS,* 10.65), so that Bloom's "laying hand to jaw" (*U,* 390.16) can be taken as a reference to either month or to both.

Gilbert has previously warned that "The growth of an embryo is not uniform; one part, stealing a march of the others, may prematurely reach a higher stage of development; an eye, for instance, may develop out of its turn."[4] As an example of this he cites the "anticipation of an early Church style" (*U,* 386.05-08), but two "eyes" do develop out of turn on the third page of the chapter: "Light swift her eyes kindled" (*U,* 385.28), and "As her eyes then ongot his weeds swart" (*U,* 385.30). If this was a hint from Joyce to Gilbert, he might also have mentioned to him the breastbone, attributed by the chart to the seventh month, which occurs on the same page as the eyes: "Christ's rood made she on breastbone" (*U,* 385.18-19).

There are several such misplaced embryological correspondences in this chapter, indicating that Joyce was either being willfully perverse or, what is more likely, that after sketching out a nine-month framework to his satisfaction, he proceeded to write a chapter of a novel, refusing to subordinate artistic concerns to extra-literary devices. The embryological terminology and references, like the Homeric parallels throughout *Ulysses,* are only a point of departure, a frame of reference around which a narrative can be organized and from which an expressive texture can be derived.

It is as a chapter of a novel that Stanley Sultan, in his *The Argument of Ulysses*, discusses the "Oxen of the Sun." Rather than dividing the nine parts of the chapter on the basis of embryological references, he finds "nine distinct phases" in the action:

> The first is Bloom's arrival at the hospital on Holles Street and the invitation to the party. The second is a description of the party. The third is devoted to Stephen and his pronouncements and ends with the Bunyanesque condemnation of him and all the others. The fourth is a short recapitulation of the situation in the language of "Pepys-Evelyn." The fifth is the "bull" discussion. . . .
>   The sixth "part" of the action is the flippant and therefore blasphemous talk about sex, and is appropriately initiated by Mulligan's arrival at the gathering. The seventh is the discussion of childbirth and of abnormal infants and is initiated by the announcement of the birth of the Purefoy baby. The eighth deals with Mrs. Purefoy and her baby and Bloom's memory of Stephen as a little boy. The last begins with Stephen's shouted "Burke's!" and comprises the departure for Burke's public house, the drinking and conversation there, and the dissolution of the group after the bar closes.[5]

Sultan's arrangement of the parts of this chapter is a reasonable and "natural delineation of its action" and contributes to an understanding of the plot, but the fact remains that Joyce did consult a gestation chart while writing the chapter and took copious notes on the characteristics of the developing human embryo which he evidently felt were reflected in his writing.

The most complete, and most frequently cited, study of the "Oxen of the Sun," by A. M. Klein, is based on the assumption that the embryological references are significant and that they form a coherent pattern. Klein does include a *caveat* in his article:

> It should be stated here, to avail throughout, that often the point where one month ends and the other begins cannot be indicated with precision. These liminal ambiguities, moreover, are intentional; it is "a nine-parted episode *without divisions*" that Joyce is writing; and he writes thus to imitate embryological life where the indicia of the second month, for example, do not always wait for a complete lunar revolution to elapse before they make themselves manifest. Sometimes they come earlier, sometimes later, but in the general nine-month progression they are identifiable month by month.[6]

The first month, according to Klein, is indicated by the presence of Bloom (sperm), nurse Callan (ovum), and the cervix, suggested by the name of Sir Andrew Horne, "Horne, that is to say, an inlet of the sea (cf. Golden Horn)" (p. 29). The cell division resulting in the development of the blastula is effected by "a warlock with his breath that he blares into them like to bubbles" ([*U*, 387.10–11] Klein, p. 29).

The next two months are "explicitly indicated," the second by the statement that "'at the end of the second month a human soul was infused' [*U*, 390.08–09], but the month—as will be seen later from the chapter-correspondences—goes back to the previous page where references to the 'cup' show that invagination preliminary to the fashioning of the gastrula has taken place" (Klein, p. 29). Also in the second month, "the head of the embryo is disproportionately large.... External genitalia appear, but sex cannot be differentiated" (p. 30). For this last characteristic Klein gives what is to me a rather cryptic correspondence: "and nature has other ends than we. Then said Dixon junior to Punch Costello wist he what ends" [*U,* 389.26-28] (p. 30). The third month is likewise "explicitly announced in Punch Costello's song: '*The first three months she was not well, Staboo*' [*U,* 392.07-08], but the month begins earlier on P:[390]. This is the month when centres of ossification appear: 'A wariness of mind he would answer as fitted all and, laying hand to jaw'" (p. 30).

Klein has only one correspondence for the fourth month. "This is not named by number; it is, however, the month in which sex can be differentiated; hence the 'anthem *Ut novetur sexus omnis corporis mysterium*' [*U,* 393.01-02]" (p. 30). Unfortunately for Klein's thesis, according to Joyce's chart sexual differentiation occurs in the third, not the fourth month. In the fifth, "heart sounds are for the first time perceptible" and "foetal movements are usually felt by the mother" (p. 30). There are no references in Joyce's notes to "heart sounds," but "foetal movements," properly assigned by Klein to the fifth month, may be associated with less strain to the "knocks" of the Purefoy baby (*U,* 397.35), than with Klein's "post-natal womb-acrobatics...Pickaback and Topsyturvy and Shameface (the typical embryonic attitude) and Cheek by Jowl" (p. 30).

Klein bases his identification of the sixth month on another cryptic allusion, "Mal M's brother will stay a month" [*U,* 397.16-17], and on "the reference to children dying at birth:" 'Tis her ninth chick to live' [*U,* 397.36]. If born during the sixth month, fetus never survives" (p. 30). That the fetus can survive, however, during the seventh month "is alluded to when my Lord Harry, in a totally different context, 'slapped...posteriors very soundly' [*U,* 400.03-04].... One descries the babe's appearance, moreover, in the characterization of the Scotch student: 'a little fume of a fellow' [*U,* 404.12]" (p. 30). This month, like the second and third, is also explicitly indicated in the text: "On P:[400] one reads of the 'old whoremaster that kept seven trulls in his house,' on P:[405] It pours 'seven showers,' and on P:[406] Kitty has been 'wardmaid these seven months'" (p. 30).

The eighth month is the "little old man month" during which the child may also be born and live, "Hence the discussion of infant mortality on P:[418], on the 'seemingly healthy child' [*U,* 419.28-29], and on 'staggering bob' [*U,* 420.07-08]—the flesh of a calf newly dropped from its mother" (p. 30). Again, unfortunately for Klein's thesis, Joyce's chart lists "old face" as a characteristic of the seventh month and "face younger" for the eighth. Klein does not seem to be disturbed by the fact that discussion of infant mortality, here used to show that a child may be born and live at this stage of gestation, appeared only a few paragraphs before in his article to indicate the fact that if a fetus is born during the sixth month, it never survives. Nor does he seem to notice that the phrases "seemingly healthy child" and "staggering bob" are to be found in what he calls the ninth month. The ninth month itself is identified only by references to the number nine, which Klein himself admits "abound throughout *Ulysses* in general and *The Oxen of the Sun* in particular" (pp. 30–31), and by references to birth.

Under close examination, much of Klein's argument tends to dissolve. Although I agree that three of the months (the second, third, and seventh) are explicitly announced in the text, the characteristics for two of his divisions (the fourth and eighth) do not agree with Joyce's chart or notes, and the identification of three other months (the sixth, eighth, and ninth) depends in large measure on references to birth and infant mortality, two themes that are basic to this chapter and reiterated throughout. For example, in the first two pages of narrative following the "Tacitean-Sallustian prelude," the following references to possible births occur: "bring forth bairns hale" (*U,* 385.07–08), "every man that is born of woman for as he came naked forth from his mother's womb" (*U,* 386.06–07), "she had seen many births of women" (*U,* 386.14–15). One can just as easily find references to infant mortality in the early pages of the chapter: "the wife should live and the babe to die" (*U,* 389.10–11), "an only manchild which on his eleventh day on live had died" (*U,* 390.31–12), or in the last pages: "culminating in the exposure of newborn infants, the practice of criminal abortion or in the atrocious crime of infanticide" (*U,* 419.11–13). With criteria such as Klein's one can prove almost any correspondence dictated by fancy.

Regarding several of Klein's other correspondences, however, one must admit that, whether they agree with Joyce's notes or not, the references seem somewhat plausible (e.g. the breath of the warlock swelling up the blastula). As noted above, however, in connection with Gilbert's tentative analysis, embryological references seem to be misplaced throughout this chapter and it is doubtful whether a completely reliable nine-month progression can be constructed using only the characteristics of fetal growth as guidelines.

Fortunately for the purposes of this study, however, it is not necessary to rely completely on these data. In the Buffalo Joyce collection at the Lockwood Memorial Library are six notebooks containing the manuscript of the "Oxen of the Sun." Peter Spielberg, who catalogued the Buffalo collection, describes these manuscripts as "portions of the same draft (numbered I, II, IV, VI, VII, VIII, by Joyce; the missing portions of this draft, III, V, IX, etc. are not part of this collection and are either lost or destroyed)."[7] Each notebook is only partially filled and corresponds closely to the printed version of the text. Although Spielberg hypothesizes ten parts to the draft (basing his supposition on the mistaken impression that each notebook "represents about 4½ pages of the 45-page episode"),[8] it is more likely that Joyce entered in each notebook what he considered to be a single month of the nine-month progression.

The first notebook in the collection corresponds to that part of the text which narrates Bloom's arrival at the hospital and the conversation with Miss Callan (*U*, 385.03–386.22), the next to Bloom's entrance into the common room, the description of the table setting, and the childbirth discussion, at the end of which Bloom thinks of Stephen as a prodigal son (*U*, 386.23–391.02). In the fourth Stephen's fall from grace is recounted, and he and his friends are condemned for their sins (*U*, 395.16–396.27). The description of Lenehan and the "bull" discussion comprise notebook VI (*U*, 398.10–401.30), and the Purefoy baby is born, with ringing of bells, in VII (*U*, 401.31–407.14). The last begins with the description of Bloom's annoyance at Costello's crudeness and ends with his mystical vision (*U*, 407.15–414.41).[9]

The contents of the first two of the three missing notebooks (III and V) can easily be surmised since they obviously fill isolated gaps in the manuscript. The ninth part of the chapter, however, presents more of a problem. In a letter to Harriet Shaw Weaver, Joyce described the "Oxen of the Sun" as containing "nine circles of development (enclosed between the headpiece and tailpiece of opposite chaos),"[10] indicating that the "prelude" with which the chapter begins and the "frightful jumble" of language with which it closes are not to be included in any computation of a nine-month progression. The ninth part would thus seem to include the text from "Francis was reminding Stephen of years before" (*U*, 414.42), to "Per Deam Partulam et Pertundam nunc est bibendum!" (*U*, 424.17–18). On the other hand, there also seems to be an indication of a birth when Stephen shouts "Burke's!" (*U*, 423.01) and leads his friends out of the hospital. The problem of where to end this month will be discussed in more detail below.

It will be noted that the months are not all the same length: the first, fourth, and fifth, are only one and one-half pages long; the sixth, three and one-half; the second and third, four and one-half; the seventh, five and one-half; the eighth, seven and one-half; and the ninth, nine and one-half. The "headpiece" contains two pages, the "tailpiece" four. That the divisions vary in length, and that the variations in length do not form a consistent pattern indicates that there is no relationship in the nine-month structure between number of pages and duration, and illustrates Joyce's organic, rather than mechanical, use of his framework.

Using the divisions of the Buffalo manuscript as a basis for the nine-month structure, it is possible to find in the British Museum notesheets characteristics of human embryonic growth which correspond to the proper month of the text. My selection is admittedly exclusive, as can easily be seen by reference to the list of correspondences in Appendix A below, but it will produce at least a somewhat coherent pattern.

In his letter to Budgen, Joyce identified the "prelude" as "the unfertilized ovum."[11] On the sheets he describes the egg as having both "male & female content (epicene)" (NS, 18.38). Accordingly, the "prelude" contains both Anglo-Saxon (masculine) words such as "that," "is," and "little" (*U,* 383.09), and Latinate (feminine) words as "Universally," "person's," "acumen," "esteemed," and "very" (*U,* 383.09). One can also find traces of Anglo-Saxon alliteration: "far forward" (*U,* 383.17), "sedulously set" (*U,* 384.03), and "been begun" (*U,* 384.29); and of the compound words so typical of Germanic tongues: "downwardtending" (*U,* 383.24), "plaguegraves" (*U,* 384.02), and "allhardest" (*U,* 384.14). The primary characteristic of the "ovum," of course, is the disregard of "normal" modern English word order, more typical of the Latinate than of the English or other Germanic languages. It may be argued that Old English, like Latin, was a synthetic language, but even a brief exposure to early English texts will show that, despite the extensive use of inflections, Old English word order is much closer to modern English than to other synthetic languages such as Latin.

Joyce has also written that the "egg descending clothes itself in decidua" (NS, 18.61). The decidua, that mucous membrane lining the womb which receives and helps to sustain the fertilized egg and developing embryo, is probably reflected in the lines, "A couch by midwives attended with wholesome food reposeful cleanest swaddles as though forthbringing were now done and by wise foresight set: but to this no less of what drugs there is need and surgical implements which are pertaining to her case" (*U,* 384.33–38).

Having described the ovum, we may turn to the sperm, which is many times smaller than the egg. Joyce gives us a picture of the sperm in the two Anglo-Saxon sentences, "Before born babe bliss had. Within womb won he worship" (*U,* 384.32). The Anglo-Saxon sperm is one line long, the Latinate egg which precedes it is 64 lines long, the smaller egg which follows is 11 lines long. Bloom also is the sperm who "over land and seafloor nine year had long outwandered" (*U,* 384.24–25), corresponding to Joyce's note "spermatazoa — upstream contr. gravity" (NS, 10.54).

Joyce seems to have taken great pains to emphasize the point at which the "male pronucleus and female do fuse" (NS, 18.18). The first indication that the union of sperm and egg is taking place is depicted in terms of language: Anglo-Saxon sperm ("Before born...won he worship") meets

Latinate egg ("A couch by midwives attended...her term up" [*U,* 384.33–385.02]), and fuses in the sentence "Whatever in that one case done commodiously done was" (*U,* 384.33). That this is a point of fusion is suggested by the alliteration in "Whatever...was," "case...commodiously," and "done...done," the Latinate word "commodiously," and the coordination of the two word groups, "Whatever in that one case done," and "commodiously done" by the single copulative verb "was."

A second fusion occurs when Bloom enters the hospital. The "levin leaping [which] lightens in eyeblink Ireland's westward welkin" (*U,* 385.16–17) when Bloom enters is not quite, as Hugh Kenner suggests, the lightning flash of conception,[12] but a danger which some sperms have to face in reaching their destination, according to Joyce's note, "electric discharge kills sperm" (NS, 10.55). But the lightning does, of course, cause the ovum to draw the sperm to her, "that he would rathe infare under her thatch" (*U,* 385.19–20), so that it does occur at the moment of conception. At the level of plot action, this is the moment at which nurse Callan convinces Bloom that he should come into the hospital out of the impending rain, and if "Bloom is the spermatozoon, the hospital the womb, the nurse the ovum," the meeting of sperm and ovum is again suggested. The sexual connotations of "thatch" are obvious. Also relevant to nurse Callan's action is Joyce's note: "womb—suction—she knows" (NS, 18.10). Another indication that the sperm has reached its destination is the description of Bloom, "in held hat staring" (*U,* 386.02–03), "hat" being a slang term for vagina.[13]

In another note Joyce has listed the progression, "meetpoint, ovary, tube, womb" (NS, 18.12). The meetpoint has been indicated above. The ovary is perhaps suggested by the "terrestrial orb" (*U,* 384.39), which reaches a state of "tumescence" (*U,* 384.41), and, "her term up" (*U,* 385.01–02), discharges an ovum into the fallopian tube. This reading is perhaps somewhat removed from the original context, but I can find no other correspondence to "ovary" at this point in the text.

The "tube" is less difficult to locate since Joyce has identified it in the note "Fallopian tube (hall)" (NS, 2.106). The idea of Bloom and nurse Callan discussing the fate of Doctor O'Hare and the bow which Bloom had neglected to doff once in "townhithe meeting" (*U,* 385.25–26), while wandering down a fallopian tube to a restingplace in the womb, must have gratified Joyce's sense of humor while he was writing this part of the chapter.

Another note gives the time spent in the tube: "12 days trip from ovary to womb after left follicle" (NS, 18.39). Counting from the very beginning of the chapter ("*Deshil Holles Eamus*" [*U,* 383.01]), the thirteenth paragraph contains the reference "as he came naked forth from his mother's womb" (*U,* 386.07), indicating that a twelve-day trip has elapsed. On the other hand, counting from the beginning of the "ovum" section ("Universally that person's acumen" [*U,* 383.09]), at the end of the twelfth paragraph one finds Bloom entering the room where the medical students are drinking: "And the traveller Leopold went into the castle for to rest him a space being sore of limb after many marches environing in divers lands and sometimes venery" (*U,* 386.41–387.02).

It may be objected that Bloom, having entered the hospital, has already entered the womb. Perhaps for those, like myself, with small biology and less embryology, the following oversimplified explanation may help to clarify matters. The human embryo is contained in a sac-like membrane called the amnion, which is filled with amniotic fluid and helps to protect the embryo by cushioning it from any unexpected shocks. The amnion sac is, in turn, surrounded by a membrane called the chorion, which rests against the wall of the uterus, the womb proper. One is thus presented with an image of circles within circles, so that Bloom entering the hospital may suggest the penetration of an outer circle (womb or chorion) and the entrance to the students' room the penetration of an inner circle (chorion or amnion).[14]

It should be evident from the foregoing discussion of the conception and implantation of the embryo in the womb that Joyce uses clusters of images, rather than a series of clear, but mechanical, references to suggest embryological processes and stages of growth. The correspondences for the months themselves are less complicated with fewer repetitions and less overlay.

During the first month of development the embryo is wormlike, according to Joyce's chart. The vermiform shape, like the meetpoint of sperm and egg, is represented pictographically. A worm characteristically has a segmented body, that is, a body composed of a number of separate units which are joined together, chainlike, along the length of the worm. Joyce reproduces this characteristic by linking together the first five paragraphs of the first month, repeating a phrase from the end of one paragraph in the beginning of the following paragraph. The first and second paragraphs are joined by the words "that house" (italics mine): "Stark ruth of man his errand that him lone led till *that house.* Of *that house* A. Horne is lord" (*U,* 385.05–07). The second and third are joined "for Horne holding *wariest ward.* In *ward wary* the watcher hearing come that man" (*U,* 385.12–14). The third and fourth are joined "That man her will wotting worthful went in *Horne's house.* Loth to irk in *Horne's hall* hat holding the seeker stood" (*U,* 385.20–22). The linking words in the fourth and fifth paragraphs are slightly farther apart: "Light swift *her eyes* kindled, bloom of blushes his word winning. As *her eyes* then ongot his weeds swart therefore sorrow she feared" (*U,* 385.28–31). The fifth and sixth paragraphs are not joined in this fashion, but the sixth and seventh return to the pattern: "so naked shall he wend him at the last for to go as he *came*. The man that was *come* into the house then spoke" (*U*, 386.07–09).

Another characteristic for the first month on the chart is that during this time the embryo is "solitary"; accordingly, Bloom is "lone led till that house" (*U*, 385.05–06).

On the notesheets Joyce has written "1st month unnoticed, fear, resigned" (NS, 4.86). The characteristic "unnoticed" applies equally well to Stephen, the embryo, and Bloom, the sperm; neither knows the other is there. But "fear, resigned" more fittingly describe Bloom and nurse Callan, who together constitute the zygote, the fertilized egg. When nurse Callan draws Bloom into the hospital, it is because "Full she dread that God the Wreaker all mankind would fordo with water for his evil sins" (*U*, 385.17–18). When she sees his mourning clothes "sorrow she feared" (*U*, 385.30–31). She is resigned to Doctor O'Hare's death, "sore unwilling God's right-wiseness to withsay" (*U*, 385.35–36). Bloom shares her sentiments as "stood they there both awhile in wanhope, sorrowing one with another" (*U*, 386.03–04).

Joyce has also noted that during the third week in the womb the embryo begins to develop rudimentary limbs (NS, 12.79), which is reflected in the limbs of Doctor O'Hare being annointed with "sick men's oil" (*U*, 385.39).

The second month is difficult to miss, since it is announced by name: "at the end of the second month a soul was infused" (*U*, 390.08–09). During this time, according to the chart, the embryo has a "big head." In their argument about whether, if a pregnant woman is in danger of death, a doctor should attempt to save the life of the mother rather than the child, the students "waxed hot upon that head" (*U*, 389.11).

It is in the second month that the spleen is developed (NS, 12.78), indicated in the text by Costello's "spleen of lustihead" (*U*, 389.31–32), which may also correspond to the note, "Costello big head" (NS, 12.45).

In another note, not actually an embryological correspondence, Joyce has written "LB other son? (6th week)" (NS, 8.121). Almost at the end of the second month, "sir Leopold that had of his body no manchild for an heir looked upon him his friend's son and was shut up in sorrow for his forepassed happiness" (*U*, 390.37–39). It had been stated earlier that Bloom "bore fast friendship to Sir Simon and to this his son young Stephen" (*U*, 388.30–31), but this reference does not have the poignant connotation of "other son" that the later one does.

A reference which overlaps the first and second months, and which seems to have been condensed into the second month alone, describes the early stages in the development of the heart: "(3 wk.) 2 cavities (fish heart)

2 ventric. (reptile heart) 7 wk" (NS, 12.66–67). In the description of the table laid out for the feast is found a can of sardines, "strange fishes withouten heads. . . . And these fishes lie in an oily water brought there from Portugal land" (*U,* 387.14, 16–17). The fish image is a polysemous one, suggesting both the earliest stage of the development of the human heart and the embryo floating in amniotic fluid. In addition, it corresponds to yet another characteristic of the second month embryo, which like a fish, has a notochord rather than a vertebral spinal column (NS, 12.38). The reptile heart follows immediately with the "serpents," which have been taught "to entwine themselves up on long sticks out of the ground and of the scales of these serpents they brew out a brewage like a mead" (*U,* 387.23–25). The snake of Eden, the demon drink and the caduceus, symbol of the physician, might also be seen combined in this Mandevillean exaggeration.

Bloom's act of "laying hand to jaw" (*U,* 390–16) combines two more characteristics of the second month, the formation of the "lower jaw" (NS,10.65) and of the "arm & hand" (NS, 12.80). The arm and hand also appear earlier in the month when Bloom is eulogized as "the meekest man and kindest that ever laid husbandly hand under hen" (*U,* 388.12–13).

References to the thoracic ribs, formed during the second month according to Joyce's notes, can be found throughout the chapter (e.g., "Christ's rood made she on breastbone" [*U,* 385.18–19]; "the cage of his breast" [*U,* 394.41]), but they may be suggested during the second month by the "fair corselet of lamb's wool" (*U,* 390.34) that Molly made for Rudy's burial.

The third month, like the second, is announced by name, in Costello's song *"The first three months she was not well, Staboo"* (*U,* 392.07–08). Sexual characteristics, which first appear in this month, are likewise announced in song, "the anthem *Ut novetur sexus omnis corporis mysterium"* (*U,* 393.01–02), and the "hymen minim" by Beaumont and Fletcher, "To bed, to bed. . .to be played with accompanable concent upon the virginals" (*U,* 393.05–07), not to mention Stephen's "curious rite of wedlock" (*U,* 392.39) and the "bawdy catch *Staboo Stabella"* itself (*U,* 392.05).

The tail of the embryo, as Gilbert has noted, is seen in the "university of Oxtail" (*U,* 393.21), a mutation which is also appropriate, of course, to a chapter entitled the "Oxen of the Sun." Another reference on the notesheets, "3m ossif." (NS, 12.90), may be suggested by the "conclamation of the hillcat and the ossifrage" (*U,* 394.18).

References to the fourth month are sparse in the notes and the gestation chart has no entries for this period. There are, in fact, more references in the notes for the first three months than for all the rest combined. It is, however, possible to make some identification. During the fourth and fifth month the "ear hammer & anvil" are formed (NS, 12.92). The most striking correspondence to this is the thunderclap at the end of the third month, "Loud on the left Thor thundered: in anger awful the hammer-hurler" (*U*, 394.33–34), but the sound reverberates throughout the fourth month: "heard he then in that clap the voice of the god Bringforth...? Heard? Why, he could not help but hear" (*U*, 395.23–25); "Pious had told him of that land" (*U*, 395.37–38); "for that was the voice of the god that was in a very grievous rage" (*U*, 396.23–24). The only other reference that appears in this month is the formation of the "arm & forearm" (NS, 12.82), seen in the god who "would presently lift his arm and spill their souls for their abuses and their spillings done by them contrariwise to his word which forth to bring brenningly biddeth" (*U*, 396.25–27).

On the line following "arm & forearm" in the notes is a reference to the appearance in the fetus of "feet a little later" (NS, 12.83). Feet do appear a little later, on the page after the arm of the god, in a description of Milly Bloom, who is a "skittish heifer, big of her age and beef to the heel" (*U*, 397.20–21). On the same page we are told that Bloom has "dreamed tonight a strange fancy of his dame Mrs Moll with red slippers on" (*U*, 397.27–28).

The fifth month is indicated by the presence of nails on the fetus, and we are told that last Lady day Mina Purefoy "bit off her last chick's nails that was then a twelvemonth" (*U*, 397.36–37). This is the month in which "1st hair" appears. The correspondence is Alec Bannon's "cut bob (which are now in with dance cloaks of Kendal green)" (*U*, 397.14–15). There may also be a reference to "fingerbone" in the names of Mina's dead children being "written out in a fair hand in the king's bible" (*U*, 397.38–39). The fifth month is also the time at which the fetus is capable of "voluntary movement" (NS, 2.133), which is reflected in the fetal movements of the yet unborn Mortimer Edward Purefoy himself: "Should be a bullyboy from the knocks they say" (*U*, 397.35).

There is only one major characteristic of the sixth month that appears in the text. At this stage of development the scrotum is empty. This is indicated by way of puns: "with a bare tester in his purse" (*U*, 398.25–26), "with naked pockets" (*U*, 399.10), "spade oars" (*U*, 400.41), and literally, "farmer Nicholas that was a eunuch had him properly gelded by a college of doctors, who were no better off than himself" (*U*, 399.41–400.01). There is also a contrary indication in lord Harry's threat to make farmer Nicholas "smell hell...with the help of that good pizzle my father left me" (*U*, 400.38–39).

The seventh month, like the second and third, is announced by name, this time in Lynch's reference to his girlfriend at the Mater Misericordia hospital, Kitty, "who has been wardmaid there any time these seven months" (*U*, 406.16–17). This, however, does not occur until practically the end of the month. An earlier reference may be found in the name of Mulligan's "national fertilising farm...*Omphalos*" (*U,* 402.31). At the peak of the six-month oval on the gestation chart is a seven-pointed star or asterisk. At the end of six months, the uterus has expanded to the point where it reaches up into the mother's abdominal cavity as high as the navel. Although there are no explanations on the chart or elsewhere in the notes of the significance of the star, it would seem that it is meant to represent the navel of the mother. The reference to "*Omphalos,*" which has already been equated with the human navel (*U,* 38.03), at the beginning of the seventh month, an island in the middle of "our great sweet mother" the sea (*U,* 5.09), substantiates this identification. In the narrative, the "*Omphalos*" discussion seems to be going on at the same time that the Purefoy baby finally leaves the womb.

Also during the seventh month the testicles descend to the groin as "a pod or two of capsicum chillies" (*U,* 403.02-03), and "testibus ponderosis" (*U,* 403.18). Their presence in the groin may also be suggested by the reference to the "prostatic utricle or male womb" (*U,* 403.41-42). The breast-bone, which appeared prematurely in the first month, may be in its proper place here as "opening his bosom" (*U,* 404.30) and "locket in his bosom" (*U,* 405.02-03).

During the eighth month, according to the chart, the face of the fetus has a younger appearance. Corresponding to this characteristic, Bloom, "as in a retrospective arrangement" (*U,* 413.04-05), remembers himself as a boy and as a young salesman traveling for the family firm. He recalls his first sexual experience with "a child of shame," Bridie Kelly: the "first night, the bridenight. They are entwined in nethermost darkness, the willer with the willed, and in an instant (*fiat!*) light shall flood the world" (*U,* 413.29-36). But his "youthful illusion" disappears, and, in a possible reference to the fact that the testicles are lower in this month, he is told, "No son of thy loins is by thee" (*U,* 413.41-414.01). Testicles may also be implied in the "testiness and outrageous *mots*" of the students (*U,* 407.21).

The development of the "outer ears," prematurely referred to in the seventh month when Kitty "gently tipped with her tongue the outer chamber" of Lynch's ear (*U,* 405.38-39), may be indicated in the proper month by the description of Costello as "a cropeared creature of a misshapen gibbosity" (*U,* 407.26-27) and the malformation known as agnatia, "in consequence of defective reunion of the maxillary knobs...so that (as he said) one ear could hear what the other spoke" (*U,* 410.34-36). It is also during this period that one finds "caseous gloss in joints" of the fetus, reflected in the text by "that discursiveness which seemed the only bond of union among tempers so divergent" (*U,* 410.21-23).

The first characteristic of the ninth month to appear in the text refers to the fact that at this time the fetus has dark hair which is three centimeters long. This seems to have been split up into two sentences: "He encircled his gadding hair with a coronal of vineleaves" (*U,* 415.07–08), and "The young man's face grew dark" (*U,* 415.16).

Also in the ninth month the "thigh bone nucleus" is formed, according to the chart, and, according to Joyce's notes, "ossificat of thigh [is complete] 15 d before birth" (NS, 12.86). The word "thigh" does not occur in this chapter, but there may be a reference to the ossification of this limb in the placement of Bannon and Mulligan "on either flank" of the hearth (*U,* 417.37).

That sexual characteristics are complete in this month is indicated by the discussion of the "future determination of sex" (*U,* 418.19), and by Stephen's "esthetic allusion, presumably, to one of the most complicated and marvellous of all nature's processes, the act of sexual congress" (*U,* 420.23–25): "once a woman has let the cat into the bag...she must let it out again or give it life, as he phrased it, to save her own" (*U,* 420.22–23, 25–26).

Since notebook IX of the "Oxen" manuscript is no longer extant, it is impossible to state definitively where the ninth month ends, where the "baby" (if indeed there is one) is to be found, or where the placenta begins and ends. Hugh Kenner argues that the ninth month ends with "the utterance of the Word" (*U,* 422.42), forty paragraphs (weeks) after the lightning flash of conception. He bypasses the two paragraphs of Carlyle parody in his computations and continues, "What really gets born...is primarily the Pandemonium of the ten final paragraphs: Modern Dublin: the end-product of 1900 years of Anglo-Saxon culture."[15]

Gilbert also suggests that the tailpiece of slang is the "baby": "Thus, after long labour, from precedent to precedent, the mountains have brought forth—a grinning golliwog, *enfant terrible,* the language of the future."[16] If this is the "language of the future," however, it certainly has its roots in the past. Joyce uses in this section a phrase from the end of the Latin Mass, *"Benedicat vos omnipotens Deus, Pater et Filius"* (*U,* 424.25–26); parodies of two English prayers by Pope Leo XIII formerly said after the Low Mass, "O, lust, our refuge and our strength" (*U,* 426.28–29), and "And snares of the poxfiend" (*U,* 427.06–07); lines from Robert Burns' "Willie brewed a peck o' maut": "We are nae fou. We're nae that fou" (*U,* 426.11–12), and "Hoots, mon, wee drap to pree" (*U,* 427.01, from "And Rab and Allen came to pree"); and a parody of Dante Gabriel Rossetti's "Blessed Damozel," "We two, she said, will seek the kips where shady Mary is" (*U,* 428.06–07), to name only a few of the sources for this "frightful jumble."[17] And, if this is the baby, where is the placenta?

There is a reference on the notesheets, "placenta 1 lb., 1 20 c, h, 4c" (NS, 18.60) which appears in the text at the announcement of the end of

Mina Purefoy's labor, "news of placentation ended, a full pound if a milligramme" (*U*, 423.08-09), but since the placenta, the afterbirth, is usually last in the ordinary birth, this would seem to be rather early for an embryological characteristic. In the narrative, the revelers leave the hospital (womb) when Stephen cries the name of a local pub, "Burke's!" (*U*, 423.01). If this is the birth, the "baby," in terms of English prose stylists, may be Thomas Carlyle, certainly one of the muse's more eccentric offspring, although I would not insist on such an interpretation. The tailpiece of slang (and of other forms of language, as we have seen) is probably best considered as the placenta, the ephemeral mass of tissues which vitalizes and nourishes both the growing fetus and the language of his fathers, only to be sloughed off at "Chuckingout time" (*U*, 424.34), as soon as its function is completed. The phrase, "Most deciduously" (*U*, 426.04), in the final chaos may be a reference to this function of the placenta, since, as we have seen above in relation to the implantation of the zygote in the womb, the decidua is the membrane lining the womb which receives and helps to sustain the fertilized egg and developing embryo.[18]

Two final considerations remain to be discussed in relation to this chapter: In what way is Stephen identified in the text as the embryo? And if he is the embryo, does he exhibit any signs of growth during the chapter?

Most of the embryological references do not apply exclusively to Stephen; they are also apportioned to Bloom, his daughter Milly, his wife Molly, Bannon, Mulligan, Mulligan's "stud service," Mortimer Edward Purefoy, and other characters in the novel (including the tin of sardines). But Stephen is "unnoticed" during the first month; he announces the infusion of the soul in the second month, and his is the "curious rite of wedlock" in the third, which calls for the "anthem *Ut novetur sexus*" and the "hymen minim." During the fourth month he is the one who reacts most strongly to the "voice of the god Bringforth." He disappears from the embryonic spotlight until the ninth month, when it is his hair that is encircled with "a coronal of vineleaves," and it is his face that grows dark. It is also in this month that he is called an "embryo philosopher" (*U*, 420.11-12), and he is the one who utters "the Word," "Burke's!" Another indication, not included above, that Stephen is the embryo is that "he was the most drunken that demanded still of more mead" (*U*, 388.26-27). According to *Aristotle's Master-Piece*, "The most Spiritous part of Man's Seed in the Act of Generation, reaching up to the *Ovarium*, or Testicles of the Woman (which contain divers Eggs, sometimes more, sometimes fewer) secondaries one of them, which being convey'd by the *Ovi-ducts*, to the bottom of the Womb, presently begins to swell bigger and bigger, and imbibes the moisture that is sent plentifully thither, after the same manner that Seeds in the ground suck the fertile moisture thereof to make them sprout."[19] This is an apt description, not only of Stephen imbibing the fluids, which "Aristotle" later calls "Liquor" but of all the proceedings of the first few pages of the "Oxen of the Sun." "Aristotle" continues, "When the parts of the *Embryo* begin to be a little more perfect, and the Chorion becomes so thick, that the Liquor cannot soak through it, the *Umbilical Vessels* begin to be formed...." And it is Stephen again who announces our connection with Eve "by successive anastomosis of navelcords" (*U*, 391.31).

There is thus sufficient evidence in the text that Stephen is an embryo, but does he grow? If by growth one means a radical change in attitude, it must be admitted that Stephen does not grow, nor should we expect him to. It would be unrealistic to expect an overt and total change in Stephen's life pattern in the space of the one day treated in *Ulysses*, much less in the single hour to which the "Oxen" is devoted. There may be, however, some indication that the seeds of change begin to be implanted in Stephen at this time. After wandering the streets of Dublin all day, briefly meeting each other in passing while on their separate ways, Bloom and Stephen are finally brought together in this chapter. From this point on in the novel, the emphasis is not on Bloom alone, or on Stephen alone, but on the relationship between the two. Joyce has chosen to bring them together in the eleventh chapter of the "Odyssey" portion of *Ulysses*, and it is well known that the number eleven for Joyce signified rebirth, the renewal after the completion of a decade. It is in this chapter that Bloom consciously connects Stephen with his own dead son, Rudy, and grieves "for young Stephen for that he lived riotously with those wastrels and murdered his goods with whores" (*U*, 390.41–391.02), a relationship which reaches its culmination with the vision of Rudy at the end of the "Circe" episode. Bloom assumes this paternal role toward Stephen at the hospital, and maintains it to the end of the novel, following Stephen to nighttown, rescuing him from the attack of the British soldiers, and taking him home to number 7 Eccles Street to an implied communion and atonement. If the subtle changes which are later implied in Stephen's attitude, and which are the issue of Bloom's attention, can be called growth, then Stephen is at least placed in the occasion of growth in the "Oxen of the Sun."

4

The Parodies

A primary function of the parodies in the "Oxen" is to help Joyce tell the story of the meeting of Leopold Bloom and Stephen Dedalus in the lounge of the maternity hospital where they are sitting, drinking and talking with a group of men, while Mina Purefoy has her baby upstairs. That the parodies, with all the Baroque wit appropriate to an encyclopedic form, are ends in themselves, as well as tools, is implied in Joyce's ambiguous description of his narrative process in the letter to Budgen. He writes that he is recounting his story "by way of" each of the masters of English prose style, and that is exactly what he is doing.[1] Harry Levin has observed, and rightly I believe, that Joyce's "parodies reveal himself—Joyce the Jacobean divine, Joyce the Restoration diarist, Joyce the Augustine essayist, Joyce the Gothic novelist."[2] Throughout this chapter Joyce is the omniscient narrator, dipping into the minds of his characters, usually Bloom's or Stephen's, intruding to comment on the action, but constantly retaining the attitude of the advocate of fertility and condemner of sterility, whether biological, intellectual or artistic. Rather than assuming only one mask, however, as would the traditional narrator, Joyce assumes a series of masks, enabling him to deliver his narrative from a variety of viewpoints, as it might have been told by Mandeville or Defoe, Swift or Pater, had they been writing this chapter. The drunken students of 1904 might have been learning knights in the fifteenth century, likely brangling fellows in the seventeenth century, officers of state to Gibbon, parliamentary debaters to Macaulay. Junius would expose their hypocrisy; DeQuincey would give them visions; Pater and Ruskin would paint their picture.

I have been able to determine little significant relationship between the authors parodied and the months in which they occur. There may be, of course, biographical details or artistic quirks to which Joyce alludes in the text, but if so, I am unaware of them. There is, however, a connection between the theme of human conception, growth and birth in the chapter and that of artistic conception, growth and birth. In chapter two of this study I indicated in passing that the parodic technique of the "Oxen of the

Sun" is a method of showing, by metamorphosis of literary style, the successive reincarnations of the artistic Logos.[3] My assertion is based less on external documentary evidence than on a simple application of the Joycean esthetic to the history of English prose style. If the process of artistic creation is a matter of the Word becoming flesh in the virgin womb of the imagination, it is reasonable to assume that Joyce's predecessors enjoyed the privilege of a similar impregnation, and that they, too, performed a priestlike function for the literary cultus. Although it is easy, perhaps too easy, to evaluate the success with which they applied their gifts by current personal or critical prejudices and to find in Joyce's parodies a condemnation of past writers by an appeal to the latest "absolutes" of literary taste, I feel that it is more sound to acknowledge the fact that the men whose styles Joyce chose to imitate are the giants of English prose, the past bearers of the "mystical estate" which has devolved on the artistic masters of the present, including, perhaps culminating in, James Joyce,[4] and that the parodies celebrate the members of this apostolic succession.[4] Joyce may or may not have had any particular bias for or against the authors he was imitating, and if he did, I have found little indication of it in the "Oxen." Nor has Harry Levin, who deems it a flaw in Joyce's technique: "When a self-effacing parodist—a Max Beerbohm—takes off a writer, the result is acute criticism. When Joyce is dealing with others, he lacks this insight and precision."[5] But perhaps Joyce did not intend to criticize in his parodies; perhaps he was at least partly serious when he told Frank Budgen, "But, you know, I don't pretend to be a good critic."[6] There are, of course, digs at other writers in the "Oxen," but they are not by way of parody. It is not difficult to find the playwright in "Pshaw, I tell thee! He is a mule, a dead gasteropod, without vim or stamina, not worth a cracked kreutzer" (*U,* 423.37–38). Some of the "hoary pandemonium of ills, enlarged glands, mumps, quinsy, bunions" (*U,* 423.42–424.01) sound suspiciously like the names of writers: Lamb, Monk (Lewis), De Quincey, Bunyan. But these are isolated references unrelated to the parody in which they occur.

Other commentators, granting the excellence of the writers parodied, have noted the disparity between the grandeur of style and the lowness of the subject matter. But it is also part of the Joycean esthetic that the artist transmutes "the daily bread of experience into the radiant body of ever-living life" and this is precisely what writers before Joyce have done. Malory's virtuous knights for example were unwashed, unlettered feudal warlords. Although they are excellent fighters, slaying rival kings and gladitorial opponents with grace and ease, they always seem to fail in their religious quests because of their lust and bloodthirstiness. Yet they are heroes in Malory, because his art has made them so. Most of the artists parodied in this chapter, like Malory, idealized their material, turning with their art all the flesh that passed before them into "the word that shall not pass away." Both their subject matter and their styles have died away and gone out of use, but paradoxically the runes they have left behind are literary monuments, the "mansions of eternity." If there is any irony in Joyce's use of the styles to narrate this chapter, it is the irony of all art, and is in keeping with his own esthetic and with the traditional role of art as something elevated, regardless of its subject.

In an interview with Richard Ellmann, Stanislaus Joyce said that while writing the "Oxen of the Sun" his brother "kept before him a diagram showing the ontogeny of the foetus during nine months, and also studied Saintsbury's *A History of English Prose Rhythm*."[7] We have seen in the previous chapter that Joyce did use a gestation chart while constructing this episode, and that he went beyond the chart for the material he needed. We have also seen that he was not averse to using embryological characteristics out of normal sequence if his narrative or the particular texture he was trying to achieve demanded it. The same can be said of his use of Saintsbury, whose talents he evidently held in high regard. After *Ulysses* was published Joyce wrote to Harriet Shaw Weaver asking her to send a press copy of his novel to Saintsbury. "I am oldfashioned enough to admire him," he wrote, "though he may not return the compliment. He is however quite capable of flinging the tome back through your window, especially if the 1922 vintage has not matured to his liking."[8] Joyce may have been oldfashioned in his admiration, but he could hardly have found a more affable guide through the monuments of English prose style. Although he is lavish in his use of metrical analysis of prose rhythms, Saintsbury does not permit his technical apparatus to overshadow his main concern: "the final decision must always be left to the sensitive ear in each individual case,"[9] he says, and the aim of his book is to help educate the reader's ear, to develop taste rather than to inculcate a scientific objectivity in evaluation. Of Ruskin's description of St. Mark's cathedral he writes,

> Now, of course, it obviously may be said, and probably has been said a hundred times, that this is illegitimate, a "monstrous beauty," something that "you *ought not* to like." Well! this is the seventh vial-volume (I blush for it) that I have opened in hope of pouring contempt and destruction on the doctrine of monstrous beauties. It is impossible that beauty should be monstrous; and if I met a monster that pretended to be one and was beautiful, I should, like Prince Seithenyn, tell it to its beautiful face that it was no monster. But *is* this beautiful? There of course we come to the old flaming walls of the world of taste. I can only say that if it is not, I do not know where beauty of prose is to be found.[10]

Saintsbury approaches each of the authors he discusses with the same openness, commenting on his copious illustrations with wit governed by his own educated taste.

To supplement his reading of Saintsbury, Joyce turned to W. Peacock's *English Prose from Mandeville to Ruskin.*[11] First noted by J. S. Atherton and since mined by Phillip Herring, Peacock's anthology accounts for over three hundred entries on the notesheets, roughly four times the number I have been able to find in Saintsbury.[12]

Joyce did not imitate the styles of all the writers he found in Saintsbury and Peacock, nor did he limit himself to their samples of prose style. He invaded Mandeville, Malory, Berners, Defoe, Sterne, and many others in his search for *mots justes,* using the words he found in the same way he used the embryological characteristics. For example, in Goldsmith's "The Story of the Chinese Matron," he found the following description of Choang and Hansi: "They walked hand-in-hand wherever they appeared, showing every mark of mutual satisfaction; embracing, kissing, their mouths were forever joined, and, to speak in the language of anatomy, it was with them one perpetual anastomosis."[13] From this sentence Joyce copied the words "perpetual anastomosis" (NS, 14.53) and used them, not in the Goldsmith parody, not even in the eighteenth-century parodies, but in the Elizabethan Chronicle parody, some two hundred years earlier, to describe Eve, "our grandam, which we are linked up with by successive anastomosis of navelcords" (*U,* 391.30–31).

This displacement of words is certainly not the result of a lack of care on Joyce's part. He went to his sources for a vocabulary with which to clothe a narrative and clothe it he did, being more scrupulous about the texture he wished to create than about historical accuracy. For the most part, however, Joyce did use his borrowed vocabulary in the proper parodies, or at least in the proper periods, so that the various styles can be identified.

Of course, it is not necessary to know the exact source of a parody in order to recognize the style in which it is written. Stuart Gilbert identified many of the parodies in the "Oxen" and Clive Hart lists even more.[14] The present investigation of sources for the most part substantiates, rather than refutes, their identifications. I have not yet found all of Joyce's sources, but the passages that I am able to quote below provide a sufficient basis to illustrate the way in which Joyce used his material. Each parody, and the source on which it is based, is related to a particular aspect of the narrative. To describe Lenehan, for example, "a sport gentleman" (*U,* 398.15) with a background that smacks of vagrancy, Joyce went to Defoe's *Colonel Jacque,* the story of a loose-living petty criminal who, after becoming an honest success, repents of his past misdeeds. To describe Bannon, a Dublin dandy, he used Sterne's *Sentimental Journey,* the account of the travels and adventures of an eighteenth-century fop. To portray the rebellious complaints of the students against risking a mother's life to save her child's

he used Lord Berners' narration of the Wat Tyler rebellion. To congratu-
late Theodore Purefoy and affirm the value of procreation he went to an
anti-Malthusian diatribe in *Sartor Resartus*. Although the most that I
can say about many of Joyce's sources is that they are appropriate to the
action, description or digression for which he used them, this is an advance
over questioning the relevance of Bunyan to Mrs. Purefoy.

Gilbert describes the language with which Bloom's entrance to the
hospital and conversation with Miss Callan are narrated as "a hotchpotch
of early Anglo-Saxon," which indeed it is.[15] It has also often been compared to the Old English "Wanderer" poems, and the comparison is apt.
But a more definite source, substantiated by the notesheets, is an excerpt in
Saintsbury from Aelfric's life of St. Cuthbert:

> The aforesaid holy man was wonted that he would go at night to the sea, and stand on
> the salt brim up to his swire [neck] singing his beads. Then on a certain night waited
> another monk his faring; and with slack stalking his footswathes followed till that they
> both to sea came. Then did Cuthbert as his wont was; sang his beads in the sea-like
> ooze, standing up to the swire, and sithence his knees on the chesil bowed, with out-
> stretched handbreadths to the heavenly firmament. Lo! then came twey seals from the
> sea-ground, and they with their flix his feet dried, and with their breath his limbs
> warmed, and sithence his beckonings with blessing bade, lying at his feet on the fallow
> chesil.[16]

Cuthbert goes "at night to the sea"; Bloom, who "over land and seafloor
nine year had long outwandered" (*U,* 385.24-25), comes "at night's oncom-
ing" (*U,* 385.03-04) to the hospital. Another monk, (*"sum oðer munuc"*
in the Old English text) waits Cuthbert's "faring"; nurse Callan greets
Bloom, "Some man that wayfaring was. . .that on earth wandering far had
fared" (*U,* 385.03-05). Cuthbert stands "up to his swire"; nurse Callan rises
"with swire ywimpled" (*U,* 385.15). "Twey seals" come up from the sea to
greet Cuthbert; "Watchers twey,"[17] nurses Callan and Quigley, walk the
wards in the hospital. The seals warm Cuthbert's limbs with their breath;
Doctor O'Hare, receiving the last sacraments, has "sick men's oil to his
limbs" (*U,* 385.39).

In another excerpt from Aelfric, the New Testament story of the centurion, appears the following sentence: "Soothly he manifested mickle
humility in this, that he said, 'Lord, not am I worthy that thou infare
under my thatch.'"[18] Although Joyce did not copy this on the notesheets, a
parallel sentence does appear in the "Oxen": "Christ's rood made she on
breastbone and him drew that he would rathe infare under her thatch" (*U,*
385.18-20). Literally, to infare under a thatch means the same in both
sentences: to enter a building. The statement of the centurion, however, as
Joyce would well have known, is the source for the *"Domine non sum*

dignus" prayer in the Mass said by communicants before receiving the host: "Lord I am not worthy that you should come under my roof. Speak but the word and my soul shall be healed." In the "Oxen" it is a description of another sort of communion, the meeting of the egg and sperm in the Fallopian tube and, at another level, the entrance of the penis into the vagina. Depending on one's point of view, Joyce is either blasphemously using a prayer from the Mass to describe an obscene act, or to suggest the sacramental nature of copulation, that is, a visible and outward sign of a spiritual union.

As Bloom and nurse Callan stand "there both awhile in wanhope, sorrowing one with other" (*U,* 386.03–04), an authorial intrusion reminds the reader that as everyman "came naked forth from his mother's womb so naked shall he wend him at the last for to go as he came" (*U,* 385.07–08). Gilbert calls this an "anticipation of an early Church style," but it is more likely, as Weldon Thornton suggests, that this paragraph is in the style of the fifteenth-century morality play, *Everyman.* Thornton compares it to the Messenger's prologue: "Man, in the beginning,/Look well, and take good heed to the ending,/Be you never so gay./You think sin in the beginning full sweet,/Which in the end causeth the soul to weep,/When the body lieth in clay."[19]

Joyce does not seem to have copied anything from Saintsbury's Mandeville excerpt, but Saintsbury does point out a characteristic of Mandeville's style which helps to identify the parody: his writing is "arranged for the most part in very short sentences, introduced (exactly like those of a child telling stories) by 'And'."[20] Of the twenty sentences in the parody, seventeen begin with "And," one with "Also," one with "But," and one with "Thanked."

If the notesheets are at all an accurate indication, Joyce seems to have read, or at least recorded, Peacock's Mandeville in reverse, from page 5 (NS, 7.96–101) to page 4 (NS, 7.102–106), page 2 (NS, 7.108), page 3 (NS, 7.109) and page 1 (NS, 7.110), before leaving Peacock for a more complete version of the *Travels* (NS, 7.122–29).

Of the three Mandeville excerpts in Peacock, the last, "Of a Rich Man, that Made a Marvellous Castle, and Cleped it Paradise; and of his Subtlety," seems most fruitful as a source.[21] There is some similarity between the situation in Mandeville and that in the "Oxen." Gatholonabes, the rich man who lives on the island of Mistorak, invites knights into his paradise and Dixon invites Bloom into a "marvellous castle" (*U,* 386.41). But it is Bloom who is, like Gatholonabes, "a man of cautels and a subtle" (*U,* 386.36). It is also Bloom who will later invite Stephen to his home and who will contemplate an alliance between Stephen and Molly, or even Milly, who, like the damsels in Gatholonabes' garden, is fifteen years old. Of course Bloom's garden with its "scabby soil" (*U,* 68.10) is anything but a paradise and his plans to have Stephen move into number 7 Eccles Street will probably never be fulfilled. The "creamfruit melon" (*U,* 217.33) he offers Stephen is a false promise of paradise, at least from the literal viewpoint of Bloom's plans, but it does offer Stephen the insight into the human condition which he needs to rise above his sterile aestheticism.[22]

Mandeville's description "Of the Devil's head in the Valley Perilous," not found in Peacock or Saintsbury but listed by Saintsbury as a "choice thing," was also used by Joyce.[23] Although he copied fewer words from this passage than from the preceding one, it still seems to have influenced his text. Like the tale of Gatholonabes, it concerns the penetration of a marvelous and dangerous place, one of the entries of hell. The corresponding section of the "Oxen" depicts Bloom entering a "castle" described in marvelous terms. On the embryological level, the zygote is here entering the womb, certainly a marvelous place. The element of danger, however, is less evident, reflected only in Bloom's reluctance to join Dixon and the others and in nurse Callan's seconding of Bloom's apprehensions.

The strongest verbal parallel between the second Mandeville selection and Joyce's text does not appear on the notesheets: "Thanked be Almighty God" (*U,* 387.33–34). In Mandeville this is an expression of relief at having survived the dangers of the perilous vale. In the "Oxen" it is brought forth by Bloom's finally sitting down to rest after his long travels, and by the zygote finally becoming settled in the womb. It may also be a sigh of relief from Joyce at having finished imitating Mandeville. In a 1903 review of *The Adventures of Prince Aga Mirza,* by Aquila Kempster, Joyce wrote, "the people who regulate the demand for fiction are being day by day so restricted by the civilization they have helped to build up that they are not unlike the men of Mandeville's time, for whom enchantments, and monsters, and deeds of prowess were so liberally purveyed."[24] But since, according to Saintsbury, "Nobody whose opinion is good for anything has ever undervalued Mandeville as a writer,"[25] Joyce may have felt obligated to overcome his repugnance towards Mandeville's content in order to emulate his form.

According to Joyce's letter to Budgen, the parodies following Mandeville are "Malory's *Morte d'Arthur* ('but that franklin Lenehan was prompt ever to pour them so that at the least way mirth should not lack'), then the Elizabethan chronicle style ('about that present time young Stephen filled all cups')" (*U,* 389.12–14, 391.03).[26] Between the end of the Mandeville parody ("Thanked be Almighty God") and the beginning of the "Elizabethan chronicle" parody there are at least twenty-five phrases that Joyce copied from Malory. But there are also borrowings in these pages from, among others, Wyclif, Fisher, Holinshed, North, Elyot, More, and especially John Bourchier, Lord Berners. It is, in fact, Lord Berners who seems to be a primary source from "Now let us speak of that fellowship" (*U,* 388.17), a typical Berners introduction, to the end of the section designated by Joyce as a Malory parody, including the passage in which appear the lines cited by Joyce in his letter as a sample of Malory. Joyce's letter, of course, was written midway in the composition of the chapter, so that it is probable that Joyce either altered his intention by the time his writing was complete or that he never intended the letter to be a complete and detailed listing.

The Malory phrases are concentrated in the passage beginning "This meanwhile this good sister" (*U,* 387.35) and ending "Woman's woe with wonder pondering" (*U,* 388.16). As with the Mandeville parody, Joyce turned to Saintsbury, Peacock, and beyond for his sources. The notesheets indicate that he began with the extract in Peacock (NS, 7.11–42), moved to another text for the chapter preceding those in Peacock (NS, 7.45–50), then to Saintsbury (NS, 7.51–56) and, finally, to a complete edition of Malory, and to another notesheet, for the remainder (NS, 2.55–100, passim). The entries on notesheet 2 closely parallel the occurrence of the sources in the text. Those on notesheet 7, however, are out of sequence, possibly indicating that Joyce was copying at random or transcribing notes taken earlier and since jumbled.[27]

The paragraph begins with "This meanwhile," the first words of book one, chapter twenty-six, in which Arthur, now rendered invincible by having just received Excalibur and its shield from the Lady of the Lake, is challenged by King Rience, lord of North Wales and Ireland. It ends, excluding the alliterative Anglo-Saxon line, with the Lancelot dirge, Sir Ector's eulogy of Lancelot which marks the passing of the reign of Arthur and his followers, but here undercut by the Cyclops narrator's comment about Bloom, "Gob, he'd have a soft hand under a hen" (*U,* 315.20). In between are words taken from the Balin-Balan conflict, the Grail Quest, the Lancelot–Guinivere romance, and the death of Arthur himself. To some extent it may be said that this paragraph contains, through the power of the Word, the essence of *Le Morte d'Arthur.*

The themes of the source passages do relate to those in *Ulysses.* A dominant motif in both is the struggle of two male antagonists. In the *Morte d'Arthur* the noble King Arthur is set up in opposition to the evil King Rience, who is, ironically, the King of Ireland, and Balin against Balan, brothers who kill each other by mistake as a result of enchantment. In the "Oxen" Bloom and Lenehan are contrasted, the one meek and kind, doing "minion service to lady gentle" (*U,* 388.15), the other more concerned with his drinking, "a passing good man of his lustiness" (*U,* 388.10–11). The Arthur-Guinivere–Lancelot triangle suggests the Leopold–Molly-

Stephen triangle intimated, at least in Bloom's fantasies, later in *Ulysses*. The quest for the Grail may be seen in, among other things, the Gold Cup Race and the rift it has created between Lenehan and Bloom. Also, Joyce's early intent for Bloom, seen in "Sir Leopold, king" (NS, 7.47) is not stated in the "Oxen," but Bloom's role is kinglike, detached, alternately irritated by and compassionate towards the rest.

Joyce's use of his notes in the sections following Malory (*U,* 388.17–390.27) becomes somewhat more complex. Berners is present throughout and seems to be a primary source, especially from "Now let us speak" (*U,* 388.17) to "all cried with one acclaim" (*U,* 389.09). His words are mixed, however, with those of More, Wyclif, Elyot, Fisher, Florio, Holinshed, North, and others.

As with Mandeville and Malory, Joyce seems to have started copying from Peacock, this time with a list of names, "Berners, Elyot, More, Latimer" (NS, 3.36), probably taken from the contents page, then to the "Insurrection of Wat Tyler," to a more complete edition of *The Chronicles of Froissart* and, finally, to the selections in Saintsbury, the *Froissart* preface and the death of Robert Bruce.

The basic situation is the same in the "Oxen" and the "Insurrection." The students are complaining about a regulation of the Catholic Church which states that it is more important to save the life of a newborn infant than that of its mother. In Berners a priest, John Ball, incites the people of England with his inflammatory speeches to march upon London and the king in order to demand that he rectify the social injustices to which they are subject and to release them from their servitude. Both passages are concerned with rebellion against the established order, both revolts are doomed to failure. The story in Berners ends with the beheading of John Ball, Jack Straw, and Wat Tyler, and the subsequent restoration of the old order; the complaints in the "Oxen" are assuaged by drink and witty talk.

In More's "Death of Lord Hastings" from *The History of King Richard the Third,* the account of Hastings's betrayal and execution is preceded by a council of lords in the Tower who are being asked to consider the death of the Queen and is followed by a flashback to a friend's dream about the Protectour who "gave the boar for his cognizance" (Peacock, p. 21). The "scholars" are discussing the threat of death to a woman in childbirth; Stephen will be betrayed, deserted by his friends, and has earlier been warned by Mulligan against Bloom "that had for his cognisance the flower of quiet" (*U,* 392.23–24).

In Sir Thomas Elyot's *The Boke Named the Governour,* excerpted in Peacock, Joyce found a tale of a headstrong son who at first rebels against and then submits to his father's will. The young Henry V, finding that one of his servants has been taken into custody, demands that he be released and shows signs of becoming violent. Judge Gascoigne, before whom he appears, remains immovable, calms the prince by reminding him of his duties, and sends him off to prison until his father's word releases him. The judge in Elyot takes great pains to impress upon the prince that he is the surrogate of the king/father, just as Bloom is the surrogate for Stephen's physical father and functions as spiritual father.

Two notesheet entries pertaining to the judge are applied to Stephen, perhaps helping to characterize his relationship "at head of the board" (*U*, 388.23) to the others at the table. Joyce, incorporating Peacock's footnote, copied "reserved the chief justice" (Peacock, p. 24) as "reserved (except) the judge" (NS, 3.73–74), and wrote "reserved young Stephen" (*U*, 388.25–26) in the "Oxen." Elyot's introduction to the judge's speech, "Had to the prince these words following" (NS, 3.74; Peacock, p. 25) became "To whom young Stephen had these words following" (*U*, 389.19–20).

Wyclif's recounting of the story of that most famous of rebellious sons, the New Testament prodigal, appears both in Saintsbury and Peacock, with the same explanatory vocabulary notes, making positive identification of which book Joyce copied from almost impossible. What is important is that Joyce ironically associated the words of the elder son with Bloom and those of the father with Stephen. The envious son complains to his father about "this thy son, that murthered his goods with hooris" (Peacock, p. 7).[28] Bloom "bore fast friendship to sir Simon and to this his son young Stephen" (*U*, 388.30–31), "looked upon him his friend's son" (*U*, 390.39), and "grieved he also in no less measure for young Stephen for that he lived riotously with those wastrels and murdered his goods with whores" (*U*, 390.42–391.02). The father tells his servants to "bring ye a fat calf, and slay him and eat we, and feed us" (Peacock, p. 6)[29] which Joyce entered on the notesheets as "bring ye, eat we" (NS, 7.112). Stephen, in a parody of the Last Supper, toasts the Pope: "Now drink we, quod he, of this mazer and quaff ye this mead which is not indeed parcel of my body but my soul's bodiment. Leave ye fraction of bread to them that live by bread alone" (*U*, 391.08–11).

As can be seen, the Wyclif vocabulary begins in the Berners parody and ends in what Joyce called the "Elizabethan chronicle style." It spans a paragraph (*U*, 390.28–391.02) in which Bloom clearly connects his dead son Rudy with Stephen and sees Stephen as the prodigal son. Unfortunately, I have not been able to trace enough of the notesheet entries that appear here to assign, to my satisfaction, a demonstrable source. Tentatively, I would call this the Wyclif parody.

After this point in the chapter, the notesheet entries from Peacock are used, for the most part, on an occasional basis, usually in the proper period, often with the proper author, but not in sufficient quantity to provide a basis for identifying a parody.

For example, the Elizabethan chronicle and Milton-Taylor-Hooker passages of Joyce's letter (*U,* 391.06–393.41) contain smatterings of Wyclif and Goldsmith, as noted earlier, plus Raleigh, Malory, Lamb, Burton, Elyot, Hakluyt, Florio, Sidney, More, Addison, Pepys, Selden, and Mandeville. In addition one can find, as has Thornton, allusions to the *Bible,* Blake, Yeats, Dante, St. Bernard, Beaumont and Fletcher, Aubrey, Shakespeare's will, Moore, and the Mass. Considering this absence of clearer and more substantial evidence, I am quite willing to accede to the good judgment of Stuart Gilbert and the other scholars who have identified these passages.

I am more confident about the parody of Sir Thomas Browne, which has its source in an excerpt from *Christian Morals* in Saintsbury and in the first chapter of *Urn Burial.* "Assuefaction minorates atrocities" (*U,* 394.03), says Stephen, a complaint which becomes clearer when seen in its original context in *Christian Morals:*

> Let the characters of good things stand indelibly in thy mind and thy thoughts be active on them. Trust not too much unto suggestions from reminiscential amulets, or artificial memorandums. Let the mortifying Janus of Covarrubias be in thy daily thoughts, not only on thy hand and signets. Rely not alone upon silent and dumb remembrances. Behold not Death's-heads till thou dost not see them. Forget nor how assuefaction unto anything minorates the passion from it; how constant objects loose their hints and steal an inadvertisement upon us. There is no excuse to forget what everything prompts unto us. To thoughtful observators the whole world is a phylactery, and everything we see an item of the wisdom, power, or goodness of God.[30]

Browne is warning against the dangers of spiritual dryness, against the sterility of a formalistic religious observance. For Stephen, too, the sources of spiritual life and light have been quenched. He seems to bewail the fact that his soul is "folding back upon itself, fading slowly, quenching its own lights and fires. They were quenched and the cold darkness filled chaos" (*P,* 103.17–19). He may also be indicting the blindness of Ireland, his homeland which has betrayed him, her true prophet.

There is a passage in *Urn Burial* which Joyce may have seen and which is similar to the imitation in the "Oxen" in thought, if not in wording. Describing the different kinds of burial urns, Browne writes, "the common form with necks was a proper figure, making our last bed like our first; nor much unlike the Urnes of our Nativity, while we lay in the nether part of the Earth, and inward vault of our Microcosme."[31] Joyce took his words, however, from earlier in the work, where Browne summarizes the historical modes of burial among the Romans and the Jews. As if forcibly to make birth resemble death, Joyce turns Brown's "fasciations and bands of death" overcome by Jesus at the Resurrection into "a bed of fasciated wattles" (*U,* 394.16), the first crib of Moses, a conceit worthy of Browne himself.[32]

Immediately before the Bunyan parody, and somewhat different stylistically, is a paragraph in which Stephen, who imagines "that there is a malevolent reality behind those things I say I fear" (*P*, 243.20–21), is startled by a clap of thunder. The passage is reminiscent of one in *Pilgrim's Progress* in which Christian meets a man who has just dreamed of the last judgment:

> This night, as I was in my sleep, I dreamed, and behold the heavens grew exceeding black; also it thundered and lightened in most fearful wise, that it put me into an agony. So I looked up in my dream and saw the clouds rack at an unusual rate, upon which I heard a great sound of a trumpet and saw also a man sit upon a cloud, attended with the thousands of heaven.... I also sought to hide myself, but I could not, for the man that sat upon the cloud still kept his eye upon me; my sins also came into my mind, and my conscience did accuse me on every side.[33]

The "black sky" has become a "black crack" in the "Oxen," but the thunder, the angry god, and the guilty sinner who, not prepared to meet his end, tries unsuccessfully to hide, are there, as are some touches of Bunyan vocabulary: "he was...but a word and a blow" (*U*, 395.02–03) and "hubbub" (*U*, 395.13). This is perhaps not the Bunyan parody, but it certainly seems to show the Bunyan influence.

The Bunyan parody proper also mimics *Pilgrim's Progress,* notably the question and answer format and naming convention. Bunyan's hero is, like Stephen, a man on a quest. Christian has renounced home and family to search for the Celestial City, Stephen to become an artist. Along the way, both are subject to trials and temptations and both find consolations and safeguards. Stephen fears the threatening voice of God and attempts to hide in boasting and drink but, unlike Bunyan's sinner, is not moved to repentance. The reason for his unwillingness to change is found in "a certain whore of an eyepleasing exterior" (*U*, 395.39–40) who is a close relative of Wanton in *Pilgrim's Progress.* Wanton flatters Faithful, a fellow traveler of Christian, and "lay at [him] hard to turn aside with her, promising...all manner of content."[34] Stephen's Bird-in-the-Hand "Lay at him so flatteringly that she had him in her grot" (*U*, 396.02–03). Her behavior may be wanton, but her flattery is taken almost verbatim from the mouth of Demas, a character in Bunyan associated with money-lust, who says to Christian and friend, "Ho, turn aside hither and I will show you a thing."[35]

Stephen, unlike Christian and Faithful, is unable to resist the temptation of the physical against the celestial. He and his friends have renounced Believe-on-Me and are protected from those things they really fear, Allpox and Offspring, by a "stout shield of oxengut" (*U*, 396.17), which is what becomes, in the land of sterility, of Bunyan's "shield of faith, wherewith ye shall be able to quench all the fiery darts of the wicked."[36]

To describe Lenehan and Costello, Joyce turned to Defoe's *Colonel Jacque,* the story of a man who was, according to the title, "Born a Gentleman, put 'Prentice to a Pick-Pocket, was Six and Twenty Years a Thief, and then Kidnapp'd to Virginia. Came back a Merchant, married four Wives, and five of them prov'd *Whores;* went into the *Wars,* behav'd bravely, got Preferment, was made Colonel of a Regiment, came over, and fled with the *Chevalier,* and is now abroad compleating a Life of Wonders, and resolves to dye a General."[37] That Joyce liked Defoe's writing is well-known. According to Budgen, he owned Defoe's complete works and had read every line of them.[38] In 1912 he delivered a lecture on Defoe, in Italian, at the Universita Popolare Triestina in which he described Colonel Jacque as "suffused by... generous and sad compassion."[39] His borrowings from *Colonel Jacque* are not concentrated in one or two passages, but are taken, a word, a phrase, even a sentence at a time, from all through the book. Fortunately for the source hunter, Joyce copied the entries on the notesheets in approximately the same order as they occur in the original text.

Early in the novel occur descriptions of Colonel Jack and Captain Jack, models for Lenehan and Costello. Both of Defoe's boys are rogues, but it is Colonel Jack, as is evident from the title, that proves redeemable. Perhaps Joyce associated Lenehan with the more successful of the pair as a tribute to his original, Mick Hart, a friend of his father.[40] Colonel Jack says of himself, "I had a natural Talent of Talking, and could say as much to the Purpose as most People that had been taught no more than I.... I many times brought myself off with my Tongue, where my Hands would not have been sufficient" (cf. *U,* 398.26–27).[41]

Captain Jack, like Costello, is "ignorant and unteachable from a Child" (cf. *U,* 398.40–41).[42] As a kidnapper, "if a little Child got into his Clutches he would stop the Breath of it, instead of stopping its Mouth, and never Trouble his Head with the Childs being almost strangl'd, so he did but keep it from making a Noise."[43] Costello is also guilty of "kidnapping a squire's heir" (*U,* 399.07–08), but he is gentler than Defoe's oldest Jack, "choking chickens behind a hedge" (*U,* 399.09) instead of children.

Stuart Gilbert has already pointed out the similarity between the subject matter of the "bovine fantasia" which follows the description of Costello and that of the discussion of papal bulls in *A Tale of a Tub.*[44] Joyce is considerably more specific in his condemnations than Swift, however. Swift's Peter represents the papacy in general; Joyce's farmer Nicholas is a single pope, Adrian IV, Nicholas Breakspear, the only Englishman ever to hold that office. Swift has one Peter with many bulls, Joyce only one bull, who seems to represent all of the Irish clergy, and many Peters: Adrian, Henry II, and Henry VIII. In Swift, the bulls are driven off by English bulldogs, in Joyce they take over the country and its women, driving the men to embark for America and a life free from betrayal, oppression, and bovine cuckoldry.

Although Joyce may have gone to the "bull" passage for his content, the only Swift entries I have found on the notesheets are taken from *Polite Conversation,* and only one of these appears in the Swift parody, "Irish by name and Irish by nature" (*U,* 399.29–30).[45] The other borrowings occur elsewhere in the "Oxen," in "Circe," and in "Eumaeus."[46] Joyce was perhaps well steeped enough in Swift's style and vocabulary to construct his parody without benefit of notes. The entries that he took from *Polite Conversation* and used elsewhere are treated as units of building material, without regard to their source.

Both Defoe's *Colonel Jacque* and Laurence Sterne's *A Sentimental Journey through France and Italy* provided Joyce with models for characterization: Defoe's novel for Lenehan and Costello, Sterne's journal for the foppish Bannon. Joyce also seems to have gathered his material in the same way from both books, picking out an appropriate word or phrase every few pages, rather than concentrating on a specific passage. As with Defoe's book, however, it is possible to find in Sterne passages which are similar in content to the parody in the "Oxen." The first that I have selected concerns the picture of his beloved that Sterne's persona, Yorick, like Bannon, carries in a locket tied with ribbon around his neck.

> —I will not go to Brussels, replied I, interrupting myself—but my imagination went on—I recalled her looks at that crisis of our separation, when neither of us had power to say adieu! I look'd at the picture she had tied in a black ribband about my neck—and blush'd as I look'd at it—I would have given the world to have kiss'd it—but was ashamed—and shall this tender flower, said I, pressing it between my hands—shall it be smitten to its very root—and smitten, Yorick! by thee, who hast promised to shelter it in thy breast?
>
> Eternal fountain of happiness! said I kneeling down upon the ground—be thou my witness—and every poor spirit which tastes it, be my witness also, That I would not travel to Brussels, unless Eliza went along with me, did the road lead me towards heaven.
>
> In transports of this kind, the heart, in spite of the understanding, will always say too much.[47]

Both have left their loves behind them, Yorick his Eliza, Bannon his Milly. They are equally effusive in demonstrating the transports of joy to which love and the mere memory of their sweethearts can send them, and in pledging their eternal fidelity. Yorick's ecstasy is quickly controlled by his understanding, Bannon's by the words of Junius to the Duke of Bedford, "I wander from the point" (*U,* 405.08–09, NS, 16.26). If Bannon is indeed as facile as Yorick in overcoming his outbursts of emotion, Bloom need have little fear of gaining him for a son-in-law.

To end his imitation, Joyce used Sterne's cliff-hanging technique, the aposiopesis which concludes the journal. Here, too, there is a similarity of situation; Yorick has taken lodgings in an overcrowded inn and finds himself sharing a room with a lady and her maid. To maintain at least a semblance of propriety they stretch a curtain between his bed and the lady's and agree not to speak for the rest of the night. But Yorick, unable to fall asleep, utters a complaint. The lady answers and Yorick, stretching out his hand in a demonstration of emotion, catches that of the maid who has come in to find out what is wrong, thus ending the chapter and the book. In the "Oxen," although Lynch and Kitty are not in adjoining beds, we have seen them coming out of the bushes together (*U,* 224.25–29, 416.09–18). It is Kitty, rather than Lynch, who speaks, but the information she is about to divulge is as risque as the situation in Sterne. Lynch, too, is interrupted while telling his story, not by a maid but by the bell announcing the birth of the Purefoy baby.

I have not been able to find a specific passage in the works of Oliver Goldsmith which seems to be the basic source for Joyce's parody. The entries on the notesheets are taken from several essays and do not form a consistent pattern, but it may provide some amusement, if not enlightenment, to see how Joyce used these borrowings. I have already pointed out above how Goldsmith's description of the kisses of a loving couple, a "perpetual anastomosis," was transmuted into the "anastomosis of navelcords" linking all men with Eve. In the Goldsmith parody itself, the opening words of Dixon's outburst of righteous indignation, "I want patience" (*U,* 406.29–30), are taken from Lien Chi Altangi, the Chinese philosopher of *The Citizen of the World,* who has just been informed that in England, if a wife cuckolds her husband, it is the husband rather than the wife who is punished.

> "Amazing!" cried I: "is it not enough that she is permitted to live separately from the object she detests, but must he give her money and keep her in spirits too?" "That he must," said my guide, "and be called a cuckold by all his neighbors into the bargain. The men will laugh at him, the ladies will pity him; and all that his warmest friends can say in his favor will be, that 'the poor good soul has never had any harm in him.'" "I want patience," interrupted I; "what! are there no private chastisements for the wife; no schools of penitence to show her folly; no blows for such delinquents?" "Pshaw, man," replied he, smiling, "if every delinquent among us were to be treated in your manner, one-half of the kingdom would flog the other."[48]

The profession reviled in Goldsmith's essay is literature, rather than medicine or midwifery:

> There is a set of men called answerers of books, who take upon them to watch the republic of letters, and distribute reputation by the sheet; they somewhat resemble the

eunuchs in a seraglio, who are incapable of giving pleasure themselves, and hinder those who would. These answerers have no other employment but to cry out Dunce and Scribbler; to praise the dead and revile the living; to grant a man of confessed abilities some shall share of merit; to applaud twenty blockheads, in order to gain the reputation of candor; and to revile the moral character of the man whose writings they cannot injure.[49]

Dixon's defense of Miss Callan, "I am positive when I say that if need were I could produce a cloud of witnesses to the excellence of her noble exercitations" (*U,* 406.33-35), is taken from three places in Goldsmith. The first is an account of a horse thief: "we are positive when we say that Saunders M'Gregor, who was lately executed for horse-stealing, is not a Scotchman, but born in Carrickfergus."[50] The "cloud of witnesses" originally condemned the prior of a monastery who dabbled in witchcraft and led his followers both in the burning of heretics and the seduction of agreeable females:

> A bishop was therefore sent for, and now the whole secret came out: the devil reluctantly owned that he was a servant of the prior, that by his command he resided in his present habitation, and that without his command he was resolved to keep in possession. The bishop was an able exorcist—he drove the devil out by force of mystical arms; the prior was arraigned for witchcraft, the witnesses were strong and numerous against him, not less than fourteen persons being by who heard the devil talk Latin. There was no resisting such a cloud of witnesses; the prior was condemned; and he who had assisted at so many burnings was burned himself in turn.[51]

The "noble exercitations" of Miss Callan are taken from the following description of the "royal exercitations" of Louis XV: "Our distresses are great; but Madame Pompadour continues to supply our king, who is now growing old, with a fresh lady every night. His health, thank Heaven! is still pretty well; nor is he in the least unfit, as was reported, for any kind of royal exercitation."[52]

   I doubt that Joyce expected his readers to recognize the sources of these phrases, or of most of those in this chapter for that matter, but such incongruities between source and application must have delighted him while writing it.

   The paragraph identified by Gilbert as a parody of Burke and by Atherton as a parody of Chesterfield contains little that I can find from Burke and a good bit of vocabulary from Chesterfield.[53] The main influence, however, in both content and structure, seems to be Joshua Reynolds' letter to *The Idler,* "Art Connoisseurs," which Joyce found in Peacock and from which appear two entries on the notesheets (NS, 13.92-93). Both selections are devoted to the condemnation of those who, through ignorance or insensitivity, find fault with others who deserve admiration, not criticism and disrespect.

Joyce copied "To conclude" from the end of the letter, added "to revert to" (source unknown), and used these two infinitives to begin the last and first sentences of the passage (*U*, 408.09, 407.15). Reynolds's "To those who are resolved to be Critics in spite of nature, and, at the same time, have no great disposition to make much reading and study, I would recommend to them to assume the character of Connoisseur" became "To those who create themselves wits at the cost of feminine delicacy (a habit of mind which he never did hold with) to them he would concede neither to bear the name nor to herit the tradition of a proper breeding" (*U*, 407.39–42).[54]

The continuation of the sentence, "while for such that, having lost all forbearance, can lose no more" (*U*, 407.42–408.01), is taken from Samuel Johnson's "the depradation is continued through a thousand vicissitudes of tumult and tranquility, till, having lost all, we can lose no more."[55]

The clause preceding this same sentence, "which base minds jeer at, rash judgers scorn and all find tolerable and but tolerable" (*U*, 407.37–39), is from yet two more authors: South, "which vulgar minds gaze at, the ingenious pursue, and all admire," and Hume, "the more early part of the English History, which I gave to the public in 1761, with tolerable, and but tolerable success."[56] That the above quotations from Reynolds, Johnson, South, and Hume form the bulk of the passage Gilbert uses as an example of the Burke parody also leads me to question his identification.

In the last sentence of this paragraph Joyce, again turning death into birth, changed Hume's contemplation of his own demise from a bowel ailment, "I now reckon upon a speedy dissolution," into Bloom's anticipation of birth, "he had reckoned upon a speedy delivery" (*U*, 408.10).[57]

Like the Berners–Elyot–More parody, but in more concentrated form, this is indeed of mixed derivation. On the basis of general structure and content, I would call this a parody of Reynolds, but with the qualification that it might equally be considered the eighteenth-century essay.

To construct the parody of Junius, the pseudonymous eighteenth-century master of political exposé, Joyce collected at least fifty notesheet entries from the letters, forty of which survived to the final forty-five line parody in the "Oxen." Although most of the letters in the collection are similar in tone and style to Joyce's product, the one which appears to bear the closest resemblance is that of April 24, 1769, addressed "To His Grace the Duke of Grafton."

> My Lord,
> The system you seemed to have adopted when Lord Chatham unexpectedly left you at the head of affairs gave us no promise of that uncommon exertion of vigour, which has since illustrated your character, and distinguished your administration. Far from dis-

covering a spirit bold enough to invade the first rights of the people, and the first principles of the constitution, you were scrupulous of exercising even those powers, with which the executive branch of the legislature is legally invested. We have not yet forgotten how long Mr. Wilkes was suffered to appear at large, nor how long he was at liberty to canvass for the city and county, with all the terrors of an outlawry hanging over him. Our gracious sovereign has not yet forgotten the extraordinary care you took of his dignity and of the safety of his person, when at a crisis which courtiers affected to call alarming, you left the metropolis exposed for two nights together to every species of riot and disorder. The security of the royal residence from insult was then sufficiently provided for in Mr. Conway's firmness and Lord Weymouth's discretion; while the prime minister of Great Britain, in a rural retirement, and in the arms of *faded beauty,* had lost all memory of his sovereign, his country and himself.[58]

In both that portion of the letter presented here and in the parody, there is an emphatic attack by the speaker on the unwillingness of his victim to act in accordance with his role, Grafton to maintain order and Bloom to perform and protect his marital duties. Instead, the accuser states, they have gone to the opposite extreme; Grafton supports the unconstitutional efforts of Parliament to prevent a duly elected member from taking his seat and Bloom is guilty of attempted adultery, masturbation, and allowing Boylan to "debauch" his wife. Both Grafton and Bloom are reminded that they hold their positions only by chance; the one has become acting premier by the illness of Lord Chatham, the other holds his civil rights by "the concession of a gracious prince" (*U,* 409.05–06). Finally, of course, neither Junius nor Bloom's adversary are above making use of embarrassing information from private life to expose their targets to the full view and wrath of their readers.

Phillip J. West has suggested, convincingly, that the Lamb parody is based on "Dream Children: A Reverie."[59] Joyce did copy five phrases from the essay in Peacock, none of which, however, are used in the parody.[60] This is not, of course, to rule out "Dream Children" as the pattern. It is not unlike Joyce's practice to base a parody on one passage while drawing his vocabulary from several others and I have yet to trace all of the Lamb entries on the notesheets to their sources. I find myself, in fact, using an approach similar to West's in my comments on the De Quincey parody.

From the evidence on the notesheets, it is clear that Joyce went to at least parts of *Confessions of an English Opium Eater, Suspiria de Profundis,* and *The English Mail Coach* to write his De Quincey parody. But, frustratingly enough, not one of the sixteen entries I have been able to trace appear in the final published version of the "Oxen." The dream form, too, in which the parody is cast, abounds in De Quincey's work. On the basis, however, of the concentration of notes and the similar sequence of images, I would suggest the "Dream Fugue" section of *The English Mail Coach* as the most likely pattern for the passage in the "Oxen." In both a young girl plays a dominant role. A female child, almost hidden in mist, appears in the "Dream Fugue." She is threatened with death by the rushing horses of a carriage and suddenly disappears, as all action stops at the blast of a trumpet. When the trumpet sounds again she gradually reappears in the distance, a woman now, rising above an altar in a crimson glory. Milly, as phantom fillyfoal, is seen through the gray twilight. She, too, disappears and is replaced by a vision of a wasteland with a "moving moaning multitude, murderers of the sun" (*U,* 414.23–24) going to drink at the dead sea. Like De Quincey's female child she reappears, blended with Martha, rising as a constellation in the sky, her veil finally blazing "Alpha, a ruby and triangled sign upon the forehead of Taurus" (*U,* 414.40–41). In both, the shadowy young female disappears, only to reappear as a woman associated with the color red. Both are also summaries, in symbolic compression, of what has gone before, De Quincey's near collision between the mail coach and a young couple in a small gig and Bloom's encounters with the women in his life.

As in the Goldsmith parody, I have not been able to find a single, short passage which might have provided the basis for Joyce's imitation of Walter Savage Landor. Thornton has noted that the names Alcibiades and Pisistratus may come from two titles in *Imaginary Conversations,* but neither dialogue seems a convincing parallel.[61] Nor does "Aesop and Rhodope," cited by Pierre Vitoux in his analysis of this parody, beyond the similarity of rhythmic patterns at the beginning.[62] There is, however, a lengthy *Conversation,* that between Epicurus and his two young female friends, Leontion and Ternissa, from which Joyce copied several phrases and parts of which are reminiscent, both in tone and detail, of the passage in the "Oxen." Epicurus is conducting his two young friends on a tour of some newly acquired property which he intends to turn into a garden. As they walk, their conversation turns to death:

> *Epicurus.* Death is less than a shadow: it represents nothing, not even imperfectly.
> *Leontion.* Then at the best what is it? why care about it, think about it, or remind us that it must befall us? Would you take the same trouble, when you see my hair entwined with ivy, to make me remember that, although the leaves are green and pliable, the stem is fragile and rough, and that before I go to bed I shall have many knots and entanglements to extricate?...
> *Ternissa.* I cannot bear to think of passing the Styx, lest Charon should touch me: he is so old and wilful, so cross and ugly.[63]

We find the same juxtaposition of detail in the "Oxen":

> You have spoken of the past and its phantoms, Stephen said. Why think of them? If I call them into life across the waters of Lethe will not the poor ghosts troop to my call?... He encircled his gadding hair with a coronal of vineleaves, smiling at Vincent. (*U,* 415.03–08)

Styx becomes Lethe, but the set of river, death, and ivied hair remains.

Somewhat farther apart in Landor, but juxtaposed in *Ulysses*, are the following:

> *Leontion.* Do not, do not, Ternissa! Should that tear drop from your eyelash you would look less beautiful....
>
> *Leontion.* Some of these anemonies, I do think, must still be in blossom. Ternissa's golden cup is at home; but she has brought with her a little vase for the filter...and has filled it to the brim.[64]

The same details, tear, anemone, and golden receptacle, appear in Lenehan's description of the Gold Cup race:

> All was lost now. Phyllis was silent; her eyes were sad anemones. Juno, she cried, I am undone. But her lover consoled her and brought her a bright casket of gold in which lay some oval sugarplums which she partook. A tear fell: one only. (*U,* 415.27–31)[65]

Finally, both Stephen and Leontion have written books. Epicurus says to her, "You, Leontion,...have composed at last your long-meditated work against the philosophy of Theophrastus."[66] Vincent, acknowledging that Stephen has completed a "capful of light odes" (words taken from Sterne), tells him that "All desire to see you bring forth the work you meditate" (*U,* 415.12–13). The recognition of the young author and the use of the word "meditate" serve to tie the two passages together. In all three instances, as in the preceding example from De Quincey, there are no direct links on the notesheets from the source to the final text, yet there are sufficient entries from surrounding passages to support an identification based on internal evidence.

The parody of Macaulay has its source in an excerpt which Joyce found in Saintsbury.[67] Macaulay describes a gathering of the cream of the British empire about to witness a trial, Joyce a group of drinkers about to take part in a discussion of the problems of the future determination of sex and infant mortality. The rhythmic and verbal echoes in the "Oxen" are easily identified: Macaulay's "Neither military nor civil pomp was wanting" becomes "Neither place nor council was lacking in dignity" (*U,* 417.23–24). His repeated "There" and "There too" at the beginnings of his sentences are evident in "Crothers was there at the foot of the table" (*U,* 417.29–30) and "There too, opposite to him" (*U,* 417.31–32). Joyce combined the "grace and female loveliness" of Macaulay's empire with the "voluptuous charms of her to whom the heir of the throne has in secret plighted his faith" to describe the picture of Molly as "The image of that voluptuous loveliness which the inspired pencil of Lafayette has limned for ages to come" (*U,* 418.07–08). In both source and parody physical description is used as a means of revealing the character of individuals and the import of the occasion at which they are present.

The description of Mina Purefoy and her baby is in the style of a Dickensian retrospect and is based in large part on chapter fifty-three of *David Copperfield,* which recounts the death of Dora, David's "child wife."[68] At first glance, Joyce's selection of this episode may appear to be simply an example of perverse humor, using Dickens' words to describe a scene which is the antithesis of their original context. But there may be a purposeful intent in Joyce's application of his source. We have seen that the juxtaposition of birth and death, often the transmutation of one into the other, occurs often in this chapter; even in this parody "Doady" (the nickname for both David and Theodore) is reminded that "the oil too has run low. . . . He knows and will call in His own good time" (*U,* 421.24–26). Birth is the beginning of death; the old must die so that they may live on in the newborn. In *David Copperfield* the death of Dora marks the end of David's childlike life and the start of his adulthood as the husband of Agnes. Dora bears David no children; Agnes gives him several. It is in fact Agnes, patiently watching over David throughout the novel, who becomes his "loved one of old, faithful lifemate now" (*U,* 421.06–07) after Dora's death. In the last paragraphs of the novel, from which Joyce copied nothing on the notesheets, but which may have influenced his text, David says:

> And now, as I close my task, subduing my desire to linger yet, these faces fade away. But one face, shining on me like a Heavenly light by which I see all other objects, is above them and beyond them all. And that remains.
>
> I turn my head, and see it, in its beautiful serenity, beside me. My lamp burns low, and I have written far into the night; but the dear presence, without which I were nothing, bears me company.
>
> Oh Agnes, Oh my soul, so may thy face be by me when I close my life indeed; so may I, when realities are melting from me like the shadows which I now dismiss, still find thee near me, pointing upward![69]

Mina is a combination of the constancy of Agnes and the "pretty head" of Dora. She appears at this point in the "Oxen," and in this guise, to emphasize the fact that the sterility of adolescence must die for the fruitfulness of maturity to be born.

I wrote at the beginning of this chapter that if Ruskin were describing the students he would have painted their picture. It would have been more correct to say that he would have painted a verbal picture of them as an architectural or sculptural grouping. Joyce found in Saintsbury the "monstrous beauty" of Ruskin's description of St. Mark's and changed it into a nativity scene, retaining Ruskin's restrained, surcharged style, but adapting the content to include the oxen and the "serried stormclouds. . . impending above parched field" (*U,* 422.35–38), which he found in another Ruskin quotation in Saintsbury: "Far above, in thunder-blue serration, stand the eternal edges of the angry Appenine, dark with rolling impendence of volcanic cloud."[70] There is an upward movement in both source and parody:

Ruskin begins with a vision rising out of the earth and ends in the blue sky;
Joyce moves from the "antechamber of birth" (*U,* 422.30) to the lightning
flash in the sky (balancing the lightning at the beginning of the chapter).
Both have a quiet tension, but Joyce's ends with a more violent release, a
stylistic imitation of the moment of birth.

As the prose of Ruskin gathers to a greatness it brings forth the voice
of Carlyle in a parody based on passages from Saintsbury and Peacock,
typical of which is this paean to work:

> Two men I honour and no third. First the toilworn Craftsman that with earth-made
> Implement laboriously conquers the Earth and makes her man's.... For in thee too lay
> a god-created Form, but it was not to be unfolded; encrusted must it stand with the
> thick adhesions and defacements of Labour: and thy body, like thy soul, was not to
> know freedom. Yet toil on, toil on: *thou* art in thy duty, be out of it who may; thou
> toilest for the altogether indispensable, for daily bread.[71]

More to the point for Stephen, and perhaps for Joyce himself, is the
following:

> A second man I honour, and still more highly: Him who is seen toiling for the
> spiritually indispensable; not daily bread, but the bread of Life. Is not he too in his
> duty; endeavouring towards inward Harmony; revealing this, by act or by word,
> through all his outward endeavours, be they high or low? Highest of all, when his out-
> ward and his inward endeavour are one; when we can name him Artist; not earthly
> Craftsman only, but inspired Thinker, who with heaven-made Implement conquers
> Heaven for us![72]

It is fitting that the last clear voice before the chaos with which this
chapter ends should be that of the evangelist of work and fecundity. That
Carlyle's voice will fade away into chaos and be replaced by that of the
gospeler Dowie is to be expected and is but an application of the lesson of
Sartor Resartus. The parodic technique of the "Oxen," the perpetual metamorphosis of style, seems to be an embodiment in literary form of his
clothes philosophy, of his doctrine of *Palingenesia,* of the self-immolating
Phoenix out of whose ashes rise continuously the organic filaments of rebirth. Joyce may be hinting at such an interpretation by placing Carlyle last
in his series of parodies, out of chronological order.

The chaos of slang which closes the chapter is not all the language of
the street and popular song. Thornton lists allusions to Burns's "Willie
Brewed a peck o' Maut," Rosetti's "The Blessed Damosel," Swift's *Polite
Conversation,* and the Mass, Rosetti and the Mass being appropriately
secularized. The notesheets allow for additional identifications. "If you fall
don't wait to get up" (*U,* 425.20–21) is also from *Polite Conversation* (NS,
8.106). The "anker of rum" (*U,* 425.22–23) was originally "ankers of

brandy" being rolled on shore in a sample of Macaulay from Saintsbury (NS, 19.58). "Cut and come again" (*U,* 427.01–02) is taken from a description by John Lockhart of Sir Walter Scott slicing his breakfast bread (NS 19.103). "Allah" (*U,* 427.37) is common enough not to have needed a note, but Joyce did copy the name from Goldsmith's tale of "Asem the Man-Hater" (NS, 14.64). On the final page of Carlyle's *Past and Present* Joyce found "Sooty Hell of mutiny and savagery and despair can, by man's energy, be made a kind of Heaven" and, turning subject into expletive, wrote "Whisper, who the sooty hell's the johnny in the black duds?" (*U,* 428.08–09, NS, 20.70).

The chapter rises out of one chaos and falls to another containing the seeds of rebirth. In between are the literary monuments of the past, the historical manifestations of an eternal Word. Despite the crimes of Stephen and his friends against fecundity and creativity, the natural stages in the development of the embryo move inexorably on, from conception through growth to birth. Bloom looks on Stephen, the prodigal son, and decides to follow him, to protect him as he would his own son. Ben Bloom Elijah is coming with his "evangel simultaneously command and promise" of patience and dedication, work and fulfillment.

Appendix A

A Working Outline of the "Oxen of the Sun"

Asterisk indicates sources identified or discussed in text. Month divisions are indicated by Roman numerals.

Page	Narrative and Months	Source
383.01–08	Invocation	?
	Ovum-Sperm	
383.09–385.02	Affirmation of fertility; history of medicine, lying-in hospital. Mina's admission.	?
	I	
385.03–386.04	Bloom's entrance, conversation in hall.	Aelfric*
386.05–08	Intrusive warning of death.	Everyman?*
386.09–22	Conversation continued.	?
	II	
386.23–387.34	Bloom's entrance to lounge; description of table setting; Bloom finally sits down.	Mandeville*
387.35–388.16	Bloom meets Lenehan.	Malory*
388.17–35	Catalogue of drinkers.	Berners*
388.36–390.27	Childbirth discussion.	Berners-More-Elyot*
390.28–391.02	Bloom sees Stephen as prodigal son.	Wyclif*
	III	
391.03–392.26	Stephen's esthetic stated; Virgin and Eve compared; Costello sings and is rebuked.	"Elizabethan Chronicles"*

Page	Narrative and Months	Source
392.27–393.24	Stephen's wedding rite; Beaumont and Fletcher discussed.	Milton-Taylor
393.25–41	Stephen's reproach to Ireland.	*Improperia*
393.41–394.23	Stephen's complaint continued; birth compared to death.	Browne*
394.24–395.15	Stephen's blasphemous song answered by Thunderer.	?*

IV

395.16–396.27	Stephen's fall from grace recounted; whore described; catalogue and condemnation of drinkers (minus Crothers).	Bunyan*

V

396.28–398.09	Rain falls on Dublin; company described again (minus Costello); Purefoys described with twelve (?) children.	Pepys-Evelyn

VI

398.10–399.12	Description of Lenehan and Costello.	Defoe*
399.12–401.31	"Bull" discussion.	Swift*

VII

401.32–404.10	Mulligan and Bannon enter; fertilising farm described; bell rings announcing birth.	Steele-Addison
404.11–405.42	Bannon describes Milly; cloak-umbrella debate; bell rings again.	Sterne*
406.01–407.14	Bell rings again; birth announced; Costello rebuked again.	Goldsmith*

VIII

407.15–408.14	Bloom's repugnance toward Costello.	Reynolds* (18c essay?)
408.15–409.03	Theodore's virility praised; cuckoldry suspected.	Sheridan
409.04–410.06	Bloom's hypocrisy exposed.	Junius*
410.07–412.04	Birth announced again; birth defects discussed; Mulligan states desire for old man.	Gibbon
412.05–39	Haines appears.	Gothic novel

Page	Narrative and Months	Source
412.40–414.02	Bloom's life in retrospect.	Lamb*
414.03–41	Bloom's vision.	DeQuincey*

IX

414.42–416.34	Stephen recalls schooldays, mother's death; Gold Cup Race discussed; Lynch and Kitty described coming out of bushes; Mulligan stops Lenehan from disturbing Bloom's vision.	Landor*
416.35–417.21	"Common sense" description of Bloom's reverie.	?
417.22–418.08	"Debaters" listed, Bloom with picture of Molly in his pocket.	Macaulay*
418.09–420.29	Discussion of future determination of sex, infant mortality; Bloom quietly rebukes Stephen.	T.H. Huxley
420.30–421.28	Mina described with ninth(?) child; Mortimer Edward; Doady praised.	Dickens*
421.29–42	Impending vision announced.	Newman
422.01–28	Bloom recalls Stephen as a child, Molly before their marriage.	Pater
422.29–42	Drinkers described as attendants at Nativity scene; utterance of "the Word."	Ruskin*

Birth?

423.01–424.18	Drinkers leave hospital; Theodore's virility praised. — ? →	Carlyle*

Afterbirth

424.19–425.05	Arrival at Burke's.	Slang, etc.
425.06–426.03	Drinks ordered; Molly described; badinage.	"
426.04–37	Stephen saddled with bill; Lenehan sees Bantam Lyons, tell how he got bad tip on race, sneaks out of pub.	"
426.38–427.16	Stephen buys another round; Bannon finds out that Bloom is Milly's father, sneaks out with Mulligan.	"
427.17–42	Mackintosh appears; drinkers exit at closing time.	"

Page	Narrative and Months	Source
428.01–15	Fire brigade passes; Stephen and Lynch, followed by Bloom, set out for nighttown.	"
428.15–27	Announcement of Elijah's coming (beginning of new cycle).	Dowie

Appendix B

Embryological Correspondences

In this appendix are listed, in parallel columns, fetal characteristics entered on the "Oxen" notesheets (British Museum Additional Manuscript 49975) and the words and phrases from the text of *Ulysses* to which they correspond.

The fetal characteristics are of two kinds: those found on the gestation chart used by Joyce while writing this chapter and those on the notesheets themselves. Joyce's chart consists of nine concentric ovals with a common base, numbered from one to nine, and seems to depict the relative size of the uterus at the end of each month of gestation. All but the fourth oval contain notations of the growth characteristics of the fetus for each month of development. In addition, the first oval is bisected by a vertical dotted line, and at the peak of the sixth oval is a seven-pointed asterisk, which I believe to represent the navel of the mother. (A similar gestation chart is described by Robert Scholes, *The Cornell Joyce Collection* [Ithaca, 1961], item 58.) Since, contrary to his usual practice on the notesheets, Joyce did not cross off any of the entries on the chart to indicate that he had used them in his text, I have included them all below. Joyce did, however, cross off several of the characteristics entered on the other notesheets, and these are also listed below. The page and line references for all of the characteristics are those adopted by Phillip Herring, with whose transcription of the notesheets I have compared my own readings.

The words and phrases from the "Oxen" which correspond to the characteristics are listed in the right hand column, with page and line references to the 1961 Random House edition of *Ulysses* indicated in parentheses. Those identifications which I consider to be tentative are indicated by a question mark after the entry. The divisions of the months are based on the "Oxen" manuscript described by Peter Spielberg.

Characteristic	Correspondence

OVUM: "Universally that person's acumen" (383.09) to "had been begun she felt" (384.29–30). Also nurse Callan.

egg — male & female content (epicene) (18.38)	Anglo-Saxon words: "that," "is," "little" (383.09), etc. Latinate words: "Universally," "person's," "acumen," "esteemed," "very," (383.09), etc.

Characteristic	Correspondence
	Anglo-Saxon alliteration: "far forward" (383.17), "sedulously set" (384.03), "been begun" (384.29), etc. Synthetic (Latinate?) sentence construction.
12 days trip from ovary to womb after left follicle (18.39)	"from his mother's womb" (386.07) occurs in thirteenth paragraph of chapter. Bloom enters "castle" at the end of the twelfth paragraph after the triple invocation.
egg descending clothes itself in decidua (18.61)	"A couch by midwives attended with wholesome food reposeful cleanest swaddles" (384.32-34).

SPERM: "Before born babe bliss had. Within womb won he worship" (384.31). Also Leopold Bloom.

spermatazoa—upstream contra. gravity (10.54)	"over land and seafloor nine year had long outwandered" (385.24-25)?
electric discharge kills sperm (10.55)	"Lo, levin leaping lightens in eyeblink Ireland's westward welkin!" (385.16-17)
for sperm no gravity (10.62)	none
flagellary mov. tail (10.83)	none
whiteflower acid kills sperm (10.89)	none
acid kills sperm (18.34)	none

FIRST MONTH: "Some man" (385.03) to "childless" (386.22).

chorion (chart, ring 1)	Hospital
amnion (chart, ring 1)	Inner room, "castle."

Characteristic	Correspondence
	Fish floating in cans of oil (387.13–19).
yolk (chart, ring 1)	none
punctus (chart, ring 1)	"punctual Bloom" (423.03).
solitary (chart, ring 1)	"that him lone led till that house" (385.05)
worm (chart, ring 1)	Interconnected paragraphs: "till that house" (385.06), "Of that house" (385.07); "wariest ward" (385.12–13), "In ward wary" (385.14); "in Horne's house" (385.21), "Loth to irk in Horne's hall" (385.22).
Fallopian tube (hall) (2.106)	Conversation between Bloom and nurse Callan in hall of hospital.
womb 1st dense then spongy, ovum sticks (2.108)	Bloom is at first reluctant to go with Dixon, nurse Callan agrees with him, but Bloom finally gives in (386.35–387.02).
1st month unnoticed, fear, resigned (4.86)	Revelers do not know that Bloom is there. "Full she dread that God the Wreaker" (385.17). "Glad after she was that ere adread was" (385.31). "algate sore unwilling God's rightwiseness to withsay" (385.37–38).
soul born: conception (8.122)	"to have his dear soul in his undeathliness" (386.01).
Woman 9 yrs island conceives (Livy) (10.50)	"Nine twelve bloodflows chiding her childless" (386.21–22).
✿ —cronion (10.87)	"father Cronion" (421.19) ?
amnion sack (10.88)	Inner room of hospital.

Characteristic	Correspondence
	Fish floating in cans of oily water (387.13–19).
(3 wk.) 2 cavities (fish heart) 2 ventric. (reptile heart) 7 wk (12.66–67)	"strange fishes" (387.14). "these fishes" (387.16) "dreadful dragon" (386.31). "serpents" (387.23, 24).
3rd wk 1st rud of limbs (12.79)	"sick men's oil to his limbs" (385.39).
womb—suction—she knows (18.10)	"him drew that he would rathe infare under her thatch" (385.18–19). Dixon's persistence (386.39–42)?
meetpoint, ovary, tube, womb (18.12)	Anglo-Saxon (384.31–32) meets "synthetic" language (384.32–385.02). Bloom meets nurse Callan (385.14–16). Conversation in hallway (385–86). Bloom enters hospital, inner room ("castle") (386.42).
embryo 1st asexual (18.40)	none

SECOND MONTH: "And whiles" (386.23) to "murdered his goods with whores" (391.02).

1–3 cm (chart, ring 2)	none
2–6 g (chart, ring 2)	none
boat shape (chart, ring 2)	none
big head (chart, ring 2)	"They waxed hot upon that head" (389.11). "lustihead" (389.32). "fishes withouten heads" (387.14–15)?
sprout limbs (chart, ring 2)	"he cometh by his horn" (389.34)?
web fingers (chart, ring 2)	none

Characteristic	Correspondence
eyeless (chart, ring 2)	none
noseless (chart, ring 2)	"reek of moonflower" (390.04–05)?
earless (chart, ring 2)	none
mouthless (chart, ring 2)	"vampires mouth to mouth" (390.03)? "kissed my mouth" (393.41)?
sexless (chart, ring 2)	none
1st bone (chart, ring 2)	"horns of buffalos and stags" (387.08). "he cometh by his horn" (389.34)?
LB other son? (6th week) (8.121)	"sir Leopold that had of his body no manchild for an heir looked upon him his friend's son" (390.37–38).
lower jaw (10.65)	"laying hand to jaw" (390.16)
2m soul (10.66) soul (10.67)	"at the end of the second month a soul was infused" (390.08–09).
2nd m. notocorda formation of cartilage knobs in membrane (12.38)	Fish (387.14–16) have notochords rather than vertebral spinal columns.
2nd m formation of thoracic ribs (12.44)	"Christ's rood made she on breastbone" (385.18–19). "sore wounded in his breast" (386.30). "a fair corselet of lamb's wool" (390.34)? "the cage of his breast" (394.41). "knocked him on his ribs" (395.10).
Costello big head (12.45)	"they waxed hot upon that head" (389.11). "lustihead" (389.32).
2nd spleen — fin 9m (12.78)	"his spleen of lustihead" (389.31–32)

Characteristic	Correspondence
5 wk arm & hand (12.80)	"laid husbandly hand under hen" (388.13). "laying hand to jaw" (390.16).

THIRD MONTH: "About that present time" (391.03) to "natural phenomenon" (395.15).

9 cm (chart, ring 3)	none
30 g (chart, ring 3)	none
lips (chart, ring 3)	"vampires mouth to mouth" (390.03)? "kissed my mouth" (393.01).
sex (chart, ring 3)	*"The first three months she was not well, Staboo"* (392.07–08). *"Ut novetur sexus"* (393.01).
tail (chart, ring 3)	"university of Oxtail" (393.21).
jawbone (chart, ring 3)	"laying hand to jaw" (390.16)?
fingers (chart, ring 3)	"longing hunger for baby fingers" (420.38)?
ears (chart, ring 3)	See eighth month, outer ears. "noise that he heard" (395.13)?
3m ossif. (12.90)	"the hillcat and the ossifrage" (394.18).

FOURTH MONTH: "But was young Boasthard's fear" (395.16) to "brenningly biddeth" (396.27).

4 & 5 m (ear hammer & anvil) (12.92)	"in anger awful the hammer-hurler" (394.33–34). "noise that he heard" (395.13). "Heard he then" (395.23). "Heard?...hear" (395.25).
arm & forearm (12.82)	"lift his arm" (396.25).
feet a little later (12.83)	"beef to the heel" (397.20–21) "red slippers" (397.28).

Characteristic	Correspondence

FIFTH MONTH: "So Thursday" (396.28) to "no telling how" (398.09).

nails (chart, ring 5)	"bit off her last chick's nails" (397.37).
iris membrane (chart, ring 5)	none
1st hair (chart, ring 5)	"Alec Bannon in a cut bob" (397.14). "clipped his forelock" (400.13). "slicked his hair" (404.30).
25 cm (chart, ring 5)	none
250 g (chart, ring 5)	none
cheekbone (chart, ring 5)	none
fingerbone (chart, ring 5)	"written out in a fair hand" (397.38-39)?
voluntary movement 5th m (2.133)	"should be a bullyboy from the knocks" (397.35).

SIXTH MONTH: "With this up came Lenehan" (398.10) to *"for a' that"* (401.30).

30–34 c (chart, ring 6)	none
1000 g (chart, ring 6)	none
scrotum empty (chart, ring 6)	"with a bare tester in his purse" (398.25-26). "with naked pockets" (399.10). "a eunuch had him properly gelded" (399.41-42). "spade oars" (400.41).
down (chart, ring 6)	none
skin red (chart, ring 6)	"bloom of blushes" (385.28-29). "blushing piquantly" (405.30). "sweet creature turned all colours" (416.14). "his face glowing" (417.30).

Characteristic	Correspondence
head smaller (chart, ring 6)	none
pubis (chart, ring 6)	"that good pizzle" (400.39)?
fontanelles (chart, ring 6)	none

SEVENTH MONTH: "Our worthy acquaintance" (401.31) to "with a loving heart" (407.13–14).

fore fontanelles smaller (chart, ring 7)	none
old face (chart, ring 7)	"an ancient and sad matron . . .wrinkled visage" (392.13–15). "Lynch, whose countenance bore already the stigmata of early depravity and premature wisdom" (417.32–33).
testicles in groin (chart, ring 7)	"a pod or two of capsicum chillies" (403.02–03). "testibus ponderosis" (403.18). "prostatic utricle" (403.4–41)?
breastbone (chart, ring 7)	"Christ's rood made she on breastbone" (385.19). "opening his bosom" (404.30). "locket in his bosom" (405.02–03). "foster within his breast" (407.36–37).
heelbone (chart, ring 7)	"beef to the heel" (397.20–21)
40 cm (chart, ring 7)	none
1500 (chart, ring 7)	none
none	"any time these seven months" (406.16–17). "seven showers" (405.12).

EIGHTH MONTH: "To revert to Mr Bloom" (407.15) to "the forehead of Taurus" (414.41).

45 cm (chart, ring 8)	none

Characteristic	Correspondence
2000 g (chart, ring 8)	none
fontanelles almost shut (chart, ring 8)	none
face younger (chart, ring 8)	young Leopold (412–413).
cheeks fuller (chart, ring 8)	none
outer ears (chart, ring 8)	"the outer chamber of my ear" (405.39). "a cropeared creature" (407.26). "And in your ear" (416.10).
nails longer (chart, ring 8)	none
testicles lower (chart, ring 8)	"No son of thy loins" (413.42)? "testiness" (407.21).
clitoris, nymphs (chart, ring 8)	"flambeaus of the paranymphs" (393.09)?
sacral bone (chart, ring 8)	none
caseous gloss in joints (chart, ring 8)	"the only bond of union" (410.22)?

NINTH MONTH: "Francis was reminding Stephen" (414.42) to *"nunc est bibendum"* (424.18)? or "utterance of the Word" (422.42)?

50 cm (chart, ring 9)	none
3000 g (chart, ring 9)	none
tooth sockets (chart, ring 9)	none
thigh bone nucleus (chart, ring 9)	"on either flank of it" (417.37).
sex complete (chart, ring 9)	"future determination of sex" (418.19).

Characteristic	Correspondence
	"(an esthetic allusion..., the act of sexual congress)" (420.22–25).
nails long (chart, ring 9)	none
hair 3 cm dark (chart, ring 9)	"encircled his gadding hair" (415.07–08)? "face grew dark" (415.16)?
ossificat of thigh 15d before birth (12.86)	"on either flank of it" (417.37).

PLACENTA: "All off for a buster" (424.19) to "Just you try it on" (428.27).

placenta 1 lb., 1 20 c, h, 4c (18.60)	"news of placentation ended, a full pound if a milligramme" (423.08–09). "most deciduously" (426.04)?

Appendix C

A List of Joyce's Borrowings from His Sources

To construct his parodies Joyce collected more than 2,500 individual notes (including embry-ological characteristics) from his sources, copying them on large sheets of paper (8¾″ × 14″ when folded) and crossing them off with colored pencils as he used them in his text. In the following pages I have listed all of the entries I have been able to trace so far, giving first the wording of the original source, then that of the notesheet, drawing a line through those entries crossed off by Joyce, and, finally, the word or phrase as it appears in *Ulysses*. I have not indicated Joyce's color-coding of the entries because it does not seem relevant to the present study and because it is readily available, with analysis, in Herring. Those few cases in which my reading of an entry differs from Herring's are based on the wording of the source text and my own interpretation of Joyce's handwriting.

Individual source entries are arranged according to the page of the book in which they appear. The page and line numbers for the notesheet entries are those assigned by Herring. Occasionally, I have included a phrase which occurs both in the source and in *Ulysses,* but not on the notesheets, basing my identification on Joyce's having taken other phrases from a nearby passage.

The order in which the books used by Joyce are arranged has been determined by the order of the parodies in the "Oxen." Since Saintsbury and Peacock appear to have been Joyce's primary sources, and since they cross historical boundaries, I have made an exception and placed them first in the series. For the most part, the Peacock entries are Herring's dis-coveries, the most notable exceptions being those from pages 173–201 and 226–237.

A Note on Using the Sources

The following list is offered as a tool for further exploration below or behind the surface of the "Oxen" text. One possibility is my use of the death-birth transmutations to illustrate the Joycean, or more precisely Dedalean, aesthetic. Many others, I am sure, exist.

For example, Stephen's terror at the crack of thunder may be more justified than we realize. Behind the god in the "Oxen" lurks Bunyan's Apollyon, the angel of destruction who presides over the bottomless pit in Revelations 9:11. It is he who is in a "grievous rage" (*U,* 396.24; NS, 4.13) and threatens to "spill their souls" (*U,* 396.25; cf. NS, 4.14). Old Nobodaddy becomes a malevolent reality indeed.

In a less sinister vein, Junius' insult to Bloom, "the stuff that comes away from it is stag-nant, acid and inoperative" (*U,* 410.05–06), flows from two sources: Gilbert White's descrip-tion of the parental duties of the house martin in cleaning out a nest full of young, "the parent birds, with tender assiduity, carry out what comes away from their young" in order to protect them from "their own caustic excrement" (Peacock, p. 214; NS, 13.60), and Junius' "sickly stagnant water, which taints the atmosphere without fertilizing the soil" (*Junius*, p. 301; NS, 16.55). This cloacal transformation of Bloom's exotic balm to caustic bird droppings and stagnant water is assuredly an extravagant way to reinforce the message of his sterility and anticipates, in latent form, the portmanteau words of the *Wake*.

George Saintsbury, *A History of English Prose Rhythm* (Bloomington, 1965; first published 1912).

Quotation	Page	NS	Ulysses
"gothroughsomeness"	12		
gothroughsomeness		13.36	
Ethelbald's grant to the Bishop of Worcester			
in the stow that men hight	16		
On her stow he ere was living			385.22–23
in London town-hithe	17		
Dublin townhithe		13.37	
Once her in townhithe meeting			385.25
Aelfric, The Homilies			
"Lord, not am I worthy that thou infare under my thatch"	32		
that he would rathe infare under her thatch			385.19–20
The aforesaid holy man was wonted that he would go at night to the sea	33		
was wont that he would go on night to sea		13.15	
teeming mothers are wont that they lie			385.08
till that they both to sea came	33		
till that they both to sea came		13.16	
till that house			385.06?
Lo! then came twey seals from the sea-ground	33		
twey seals		13.18	
Watchers twey there walk			385.09–10
sithence	33		
Sithence		13.19	
Then did Cuthbert as his wont was	33		
Then did Cuthbert as his wont was		13.17	
he said dissembling, as his wont was			390.17

Quotation	Page	NS	Ulysses
Wyclif, Sermons			
And the father de-parted him his goods	61		
departed him his goods		7.119	
to fill his belly with these holes ["hulls," "husks"] that the hogs eat	61		
husks of swine		7.120	
Filling my belly with husks of swine			517.40–41
How many hinds in my father's house be full of loaves	61		
hinds in my father's house be full of loaves		7.121	
running against his son	61		
~~against (verso)~~		7.111	
there came against the place			386.25
And bring ye a fat calf, and slay him, and eat we, and feed us	61		
~~bring ye, eat we~~		7.112	
Now drink we, quod he			391.08
and quaff ye this mead			391.09
Leave ye fraction of bread			391.10
See ye here			391.13
I passed never thy mandement	62		
nor do her mandement			386.40
This thy son hath murthered his goods with hooris	62		
~~this thy son~~		7.113	
to this his son young Stephen			388.31
him his friend's son			390.39
~~murdered his goods with whores~~		7.114	
murdered his goods with whores			391.02
Malory, Morte d'Arthur			
what thou there seest	85		
what thou there seest		7.53	
Who would have wend	86		
who would have weened		7.54	
he threw the sword as far into the water as he might	86		
~~as far as he might~~		7.55	
he quaffed as far as he might			388.09–10
all they had black hoods	87		
~~all they had hoods~~		7.56	
All they bachelors then asked			390.14

Quotation	Page	NS	Ulysses
Lord Berners, Froissart			
(Saintsbury on Berners)			
especially the doublet	94		
doublet words		3.56	
they reputed him right orgulous	94n.		
~~orgulous~~		3.56	
Then spoke young Stephen			
orgulous			389.42
they were gested and done	96		
gested		3.61	
erewhile ~~gested~~			388.25
and ~~farther~~	96		
farther		3.61	
And they said farther			389.01
Mark this farther			422.29
I promised in my mind to have			
gone...sith	96		
~~I promised to have gone, sith~~		3.63	
he promised to have come			388.28
as soon as I am trespassed out			
of this world	96		
~~she is trespassed out of this~~			
~~world~~		3.63–64	
that now was trespassed out			
of this world			388.40–41
Fisher, Sermon-commentary on the Seven Penitential			
Psalms			
full courteous answer she			
would make	99		
~~he would make~~		3.66	
he would answer			390.16
A wariness of herself she had			
alway to eschew every thing			
that might dishonest any			
noble woman	99		
~~dishonest a woman~~		3.65	
he would ever dishonest a woman			389.29–30
~~A wariness of mind~~		3.65	
A wariness of mind			390.15–16
Sir Thomas Browne			
(Saintsbury on Browne)			
In admitting exceptions to			
Browne on Latinism and of			
catachresis of words	182		
catachresis		11.108	
doubtfully precious balms of			
"abbreviature" and "exant-			

Quotation	Page	NS	Ulysses
lation;" even when he has such traps for the unwary as "equable" in the sense of "equitable"	182		
abbreviature		11.56	
exantlation		11.57	
equable		11.58	
(Browne's works) terminating the acies of the eye	183.n		
acies of the eye		11.109	
Moses his man	184		
~~Moses his man~~		11.110	
Hamlet his father			394.04
Job, who cursed not the day of his life, but his nativity	185		
~~nativity~~		11.107	
nights of prenativity			394.06–07
human nativity			411.06
the diuturnity of our memories	186		
diuturnity		11.108	
the Entelechia and soul of our subsistences. To be nameless	187		
entelechy		11.59	
to be		11.60	
the Chaos of pre-ordination, and night of their fore-beings	190		
?notes of prebeings		11.59	
nights of prenativity			394.06–07?
raise up the ghost of a rose	192		
~~ghost of a rose~~		11.60	
past their first sleep in Persia	192		
pass 1st sleep in Persia		11.56	
Gardens were before gardeners	196		
gardens before gardeners		11.111	
(Saintsbury on Browne) If both verbs in the first clause had had the -*s*, or both the -*th*	198		
~~-s -eth~~		11.62	
Assuefaction minorates			394.03
Tully saith			394.04
Hamlet his father showeth			394.04–05
(Browne, Works) assuefaction unto anything minorates	199		
~~assuefaction~~		11.64	

Quotation	Page	NS	Ulysses
Assuefaction minorates atrocities			394.03
Cowley, Essays			
But this, you'll say	231		
this, you'll say		14.116	
stop up all those gaps	231		
~~stop gap~~		14.118	
ten such stopgaps			405.27
~~man in gap~~		14.119	
man in the gap			408.33
Dryden, on Shakespeare			
Those who accuse him to have wanted	232		
accuse him to have wanted		14.120	
South			
the smart of the experiment	234		
smart		14.121	
which vulgar minds gaze at, the ingenious pursue, and all admire	234		
~~vulgar mind~~ , ~~the ingenious~~ ~~and all~~		14.122–23	
which base minds jeer at, rash judgers scorn and all find			407.37–38
Halifax			
all the power upon the earth	235		
~~a power upon the earth~~		14.124	
Sir William Temple			
agitated by gentle gales	236		
gentle gales		14.125	
Swift			
a certain squabble, of wonderful importance	243		
~~squabble in womb~~		14.126	
replete with discoveries	243		
~~replete~~		14.127	
Bolingbroke, Letter to Windham			
will of the Supreme Being	258		
~~Supreme Being~~		14.128	
bounty of the Supreme Being			408.14
Gibbon, Decline and Fall			
a prince who had never			

Quotation	Page	NS	Ulysses
vanquished a foreign enemy	282		
~~conqueror who had never~~		16.44	
he affected a stately demeanor	282		
~~he affected~~		16.42	
expressed, with some pleasantry	282		
~~with some pleasantry~~		16.42–43	
in that vein of pleasantry			411.33

Gibbon, Memoirs

eloquent historian of nature	284		
~~eloquent historian of nature~~		16.45	

Carlyle

tumultuously eddy	365		
~~tumultuously eddy~~		19.91	
They are out tumultuously			423.09–10
mad witch's hair	365		
mad witch's hair		19.92	
godlike and my Father's	366		
~~Godlike & My Father's~~		20.66	
God's air, the Allfather's air			423.22
Paraguay tea	369		
~~Paraguay tea~~		20.67	
eight days' provender	369		
provender		19.127	
a modicum of pepper	369		
~~modicum~~		19.128	
thy modicum of man's work			423.28–29
all steadily snoring	369		
~~all steadily snoring~~		20.68	
all bravely legging it			423.10–11
glitter down	370		
glitter		20.69	

Macaulay

Neither military nor civil pomp was wanting	371		
~~neither x nor y was wanting~~		19.130	
Neither place nor council was lacking in dignity			417.23–24
female loveliness	372		
~~female loveliness~~		19.131	
image of that voluptuous loveliness			418.07
There Siddons, in the prime of her majestic beauty, looked with emotion on a scene surpassing all the imitations of the stage	372		

Quotation	Page	NS	Ulysses
Siddons—surpassing stage		19.132	
There the historian of the Roman Empire	372		
historian of rome		19.52	
There appeared the voluptuous charms of her to whom	372		
~~voluptuous~~		19.53	
image of that voluptuous loveliness			418.07
There.... There.... There....	372		
~~There There There~~		19.57	
Crothers was there			417.29
There, too,			417.31
ankers of brandy	373		
~~anker of rum~~		19.58	
her anker of rum			425.22–23
salted hides	373		
~~salted cowhide~~		19.133	
salted cowhide brogues			417.38
Ruskin			
its gates were angel-guarded long ago	395		
~~its gates were angelguarded long ago~~		20.65	
the vigilant watch of shepherds and of angels			422.33–34?
and the four-square keep of Granson	398		
~~or the 4 square Keep of Grandson~~		20.60	
in thunder-blue serration	399		
~~in thunderblue serration~~		20.61	
the serried stormclouds			422.35
dark with rolling impendence	399		
~~dark with rolling impendence~~		20.62	
heavy with preponderant excess			422.35?
impending above parched field			422.37–38
lulled by flowing of wave	399		
~~lulled by flowing of wave~~		20.63	
within three minute's race	399		
~~within a minute's race~~		20.64	
off for a minute's race			423.10

✕ W. Peacock, *English Prose from Mandeville to Ruskin* (London, 1903).

Mandeville, Of Mahomet
and he trowed that they had
  said sooth   1

Quotation	Page	NS	Ulysses
~~and he trowed that they had~~			
said sooth		7.110	
she trowed well that the			
traveller had said thing			
that was false			386.37–38
drink never no wine	2		
~~he drank never no~~		7.144	
he never drank no manner			
of mead			387.29–30
repreved	2		
~~repreved~~		7.145	
reproved the learning knight			386.37

Mandeville, How the Earth and the Sea be of Round Form
and Shape

Quotation	Page	NS	Ulysses
I have heard counted	2		
~~I have heard counted~~		7.108	
as he heard hereof counted			392.33
environing...unto his own			
marches	3		
~~unto his own marches environing~~		7.109	
after many marches environing			387.01
that was possible thing	3		
~~that was possible thing~~		7.116	
that this be possible thing			387.15

Mandeville, Of a Rich Man

Quotation	Page	NS	Ulysses
men clept him Gatholonabes	4		
~~clept~~		7.102	
yclept Dixon			386.26
a full fair castle and a strong			
in a mountain, so strong and			
so noble, that no man could			
devise a fairer ne stronger	4		
~~a full fair castle and a strong~~			
~~that no man could devise a~~			
~~fairer ne stronger~~		7.104–05	
And full fair cheer and rich			
was on the board that no			
wight could devise a fuller			
ne richer			387.11–13
And he had let mure all the			
mountain about	4		
~~And he let pour (mure) all~~			
~~the mountain about~~		7.103	
And the learning knight let			
pour for childe Leopold			387.26
sung full delectably	4		
~~sung full delectably~~		7.140	
drink, said he, fully			

Quotation	Page	NS	Ulysses
delectably			388.09?
moved by craft	4		
~~moved by craft~~		7.107	
vat of silver that was moved by craft			387.13–14
it seemed that they were quick	4		
seemed quick		7.107	
fully richly	4		
~~fully richly~~		7.102	
fully delectably			388.09?
hardy and noble			
~~hardy and noble~~	4	7.106	
to his desport	4		
~~to his desport~~		7.106	
whereof anon	5		
whereof anon		7.141	
In colour whereof			389.11?
say them	5		
~~say them~~		7.97	
contrarious to his list	5		
~~contrarious to his list~~		7.96	
contrarious to his list			386.40–41
for to be slain	5		
~~for to be slain~~		7.97	
for to make merry			386.34
for to rest him			386.42
for to pleasure him			387.28–29
for to rest him			387.33
any of the tother	5		
~~any of the tother~~		7.142	
older than any of the tother			388.01
most fairest damosels	5		
~~most fairest damosels~~		7.98	
in hope to have	5		
~~in hope to have~~		7.98	
his subtle deceits and false cautels	5		
~~cautelous~~		7.99	
a man of cautels and a subtle			386.36
they assembled them	5		
~~they assembled them~~		7.99	
yet apertly seen	5		
~~apertly~~		7.101	
took apertly somewhat			387.29
riches is voided clean	5		
~~voided it clean~~		7.101	
he voided the more part			387.31
And it is not long gone, sithen	5		
~~and it is not long gone sithen~~		7.100	
was couth to him sithen			386.27?

Quotation	Page	NS	Ulysses
Wyclif, The Prodigal Son			
And the father de-parted him his goods	6		
departed him his goods		7.119	
to fill his belly with these *holes*[1] that the hogs eat	6		
[1]husks	6n.		
husks of swine		7.120	
How many hinds in my father's house be full of loaves	6		
hinds in my father's house be full of loaves		7.121	
running against his son	6		
against (verso)		7.111	
there came against the place			386.25
And bring ye a fat calf, and slay him, and eat we, and feed us	6		
bring ye, eat we		7.112	
Now drink we, quod he			391.08
and quaff ye this mead			391.09
Leave ye fraction of bread			391.10
See ye here			391.13
I passed never thy mandement	7		
nor do her mandement			386.40
this thy son, that murthered his goods with hooris	7		
this thy son		7.113	
to this his son young Stephen			388.31
him his friend's son			390.39
murdered his goods with whores		7.114	
murdered his goods with whores			391.02
Sir Thomas Malory, Of King Rience			
This meanwhile	8		
this meanwhile		7.12	
This meanwhile this good sister			387.35
and every each of them	8		
every each		7.13	
drank every each			387.28
Well, said Arthur	8		
Well, sd. A—		7.14	
the which	8		
the which		7.15	
I owe him none homage	8		
I owe none homage to him		7.19	
but, or it be long too, he shall	8		
but or it be long too, he'll . . .		7.20	
But, said he, or it be long too			388.03-04
without he do me homage	9		

Quotation	Page	NS	Ulysses
without he do me		7.21	
without they see it			387.16
Now is there any here, said Arthur	9		
Now is there any here, said Arthur		7.22	
a knight that hight Naram	9		
~~a knight that hight~~		7.23	
a franklin that hight Lenehan			387.42
a passing good man of his body	9		
~~a passing good man of his body~~		7.24	
a passing good man of his lustiness			388.10–11
with a mighty puissance	9		
with a mighty puissance		7.25	
her name is puissant			391.24?
Malory, of Balin and Balan			
how each of them slew Other	9		
~~each slew other~~		7.26	
each with other			386.28?
each gen other			388.37?
by cause of his two swords, but by cause	9		
~~by cause of...but by cause~~		7.27	
by cause that he was elder			388.02
by cause he still had pity			390.28
they aventryd their spears	9		
~~aventried their spears~~		7.28	
who aventried the dear corse			391.24–25
marvellously fast	9		
~~marvellously fast~~		7.30	
that there abound marvellously			387.08–09
Balin was bruised sore with the fall of his horse	9		
sore of limb		7.29	
being sore of limb			387.01
saw the towers stand full of ladies	9		
~~stood full of ladies~~		7.31	
all cups that stood empty			391.04
all the place there as they fought	10		
~~the place as they fought~~		7.32	
or now I found never no knight	10		
~~or now~~		7.33	
that it be not come or now			387.41
to our both's destruction	10		
~~to their both's health~~		7.34	
to their both's health			388.10

Quotation	Page	NS	Ulysses
syne that	10		
Sine that		7.35	
it happed me	10		
~~it happed me~~		7.36	
it had happed that			386.27
We came both out of one tomb, that is to say, one mother's belly, and so shall we lie both in one pit	10		
~~uterine brothers~~		7.11?	
prenatal repugnance of uterine brothers			410.24?
a knight that stood afore him	11		
~~that stood fore him~~		7.37	
the cup that stood tofore him			388.07
Also the scabbard of Balin's sword Merlin left it on this side the island	12		
~~Also~~		7.39	
Also he took the cup			388.07
~~on this side the~~		7.39	
on that side the table			387.42

Malory, Of Guenever			
That is truth, said king Arthur	13		
~~that is truth, said Bloom~~		7.40	
That is truth, pardy, said Dixon			390.22
what by water, and what by land	14		
~~what by water & what by land~~		7.41	
what with argument and what for their drinking			389.11–12
rode freshly	14		
~~ran out freshly~~		7.42	
the mare ran out freshly			415.22

Lord Berners, Insurrection of Wat Tyler			
These unhappy people of these said countries began to stir, because they said they were kept in great servage, and in the beginning of the world, they said, there were no bondmen, wherefore they maintained that none ought to be bond	14		
~~because they said...and in the beginning, they said...wherefore they maintained...and they said farther~~		3.38–39	
And they said farther she			

Quotation	Page	NS	Ulysses
should live because in the beginning they said the woman should bring forth in pain and wherefore they that were			389.01–03
they would have wages therefor as well as other	15		
as well as other		3.36	
And of this imagination	15		
of this imagination		3.36–37	
they that were of this imagination			389.03
nor shall not do till everything be common	15		
nor shall not do till		3.41	
camlet furred with grise	15		
camlet furred with grise		3.41	
to the intent to be made free	15		
to the intent to be		3.41–42	
to the intent to be drunken			388.17–18
many of the mean people	15		
the mean people		3.40	
the mean people believed			389.07
such as intended to no goodness said how he said truth	15		
Such as intended to no goodness said how he said truth		3.43	
such as intended to no goodness said how he had broke his avow			388.29–30
affirming how John Ball said truth	16		
affirming how John Ball said truth		3.44	
affirming how young Madden had said truth			389.03–04
in prison a two or three months	16		
a 2 or 3 months		3.44	
the bishop had conscience to let him die	16		
had conscience to let him die		3.45	
he had conscience to let her die			389.04–05
England was right evil governed	16		
right evil governed		3.45	
the world was now right evil governed			389.06
there entered in at the gates in some place a hundred, two hundred, by twenty and by thirty	17		
a 100, 200, by 20 and 30 entered		3.47	
people came to London, a			

Quotation	Page	NS	Ulysses
hundred mile off, sixty mile, fifty mile, forty mile, and twenty mile off	17		
a 100 mile off, 60 m, 50 m, 40 m and 20 m off		3.48	
they demanded ever for the King	17		
demanded ever for the King		3.49	
demanded still of more mead			388.26–27
the good lady was in great doubt lest	17		
was in great doubt lest		3.49–50	
were in doubt that			389.05
Howbeit, God kept her	17		
Howbeit		3.46	
howbeit the mean people			389.07
for she never durst tarry	17		
never durst tarry		3.47	
sir Leopold which never durst laught too open			389.39
but the king nor his council did provide no remedy	18		
but the king nor his council did provide no remedy		3.51	
but the law nor his judges did provide no remedy			389.07–08

Sir Thomas More, Death of Lord Hastings

Quotation	Page	NS	Ulysses
that is to wit, on the Friday	18		
that is to wit		3.68	
that is to wit			388.19
These Lords so sitting	18		
these lords so sitting		3.68	
this matter was but a quarrel	19		
quarrel (pretext)		3.68–69	
as it was never other	19		
It was never other		3.70	
as it was never other			389.06–07
the self night next before his death	20		
the self night next before his death		3.70–71	
the self night next before her death			388.41–42
the Protector gave the boar for his cognizance	21		
Flower for his cognisance		3.72	
Leopold that had for his cognisance the flower of quiet			392.23–24

Quotation	Page	NS	Ulysses
Sir Thomas Elyot, Prince Hal and Judge Gascoigne			
reserved²the chief justice	24		
²Except	24n.		
~~reserved (except) the judge~~		3.72–73	
reserved young Stephen			388.25–26
had to the prince these words			
following	25		
~~Had to the prince these words~~			
following		3.74	
had these words following			389.20
shewed to the King all the			
whole affair	25		
~~Showed all the whole affair~~		3.76	
showed all the whole affair			389.15
Raphael Holinshed, Witchcraft			
to make away	29		
~~to make away~~		3.119	
his leman	29		
~~leman~~		3.119	
maid or leman			389.30–31
upon straight examination	29		
straight examen		3.119	
about the midst of the night	29		
~~about the midst of the night~~		3.120	
about the midst of the winter			390.37
still basted the image with a			
certain liquor very busily	29		
~~still basted it very busily~~		3.121	
still plied it very busily			391.05–06
clean consumed	30		
~~clean consumed~~		3.122	
clean consumed			396.33
straight ways	30		
~~straight ways~~		3.123	
delivered of his languor	30		
~~delivered of his languor~~		3.124	
delivered of his spleen			389.31
at all	30		
—at all		3.125	
was able to do any manner of			
thing that lay in man to do	30		
~~able to do any manner of thing~~			
that lay in man to do		3.128	
able to do any manner of thing			
that lay in man to do			389.37
Sir Thomas North, Banishment of Coriolanus			
to tell the voices	30		

Quotation	Page	NS	Ulysses
to tell the voices		3.126	
jocundly	30		
jocundly		3.127	
jocundly			389.38
evil hap	31		
evil hap		3.127	
evil hap			390.34–35
no manner of passion	31		
passion:		3.111	
Now that Martius was even in that taking, it appeared true soon	31		
now that he was even in that taking it appeared right eftsoon		3.112–13	
that he was now in that taking it appeared eftsoon			390.26–27
turmoiled with	31		
turmoiled with		3.111	
not gasteful turmoil			392.12
brought him	31		
brought him		3.114	
malice and envy him	32		
malice and envy him		3.116	
they did malice him			389.35
insomuch as	32		
insomuch as:		3.115	
insomuch as			388.33
Tullus rose presently	33		
presently		3.116	
presently lift his arm			396.25
bewray myself	33		
bewray		3.117	
he would not bewray			389.40
this only surname	33		
this only surname		3.117	
suitor, to take thy chimney hearth	33		
suitor, take the chimney's hearth		3.118	
pricked forward with desire	33		
was pricked forward with		3.115	
pricked forward with their jibes			389.34–35
to be wrecked of the injuries	33		
to be wrecked of injuries		3.106	
to prove fortune any more	34		
to prove fortune once more		3.109	
pleasure thee	33		
to pleasure thee		3.106	
for to pleasure him			387.28–29

Quotation	Page	NS	Ulysses
hearing what he said, was a marvellous glad man	34		
~~hearing, he was a marvellous glad man~~		3.110	
Which hearing young Stephen was a marvellous glad man			390.23–24
So he feasted him for that time	34		
~~they feasted him for that time~~		3.107	
they feasted him for that time			388.33
in the honourablest manner	34		
~~honourablest manner~~		3.107	
in the honourablest manner			388.33–34

Sir Walter Raleigh, Sir Richard Grenville's Last Fight

the one half part	35		
~~the one half part~~		3.104	
recovered England	35		
~~recovered England~~		3.104	
recover the main of America			401.26
were these as followeth	35		
~~were these as followeth~~		3.105	
were then these as followeth			391.17
shrouded their approach	35		
~~shrouded their approach~~		3.105	
shrouded in the piteous vesture			421.41?
cast about	35		
Cast about		3.91	
sprang their luff	36		
~~sprang their luff~~		3.91	
sprang their luff			401.22
becalmed his sails in such sort	36		
~~becalmed~~		3.92	
his languor becalmed him			388.32
~~in such sort~~		3.91	
at three of the clock	36		
~~past ten of the clock~~		3.92?	
past ten of the clock			397.01?
never so wounded as that. . . as he was a-dressing	37		
never so wounded as that, a-dressing		3.96	
This agreeth also with	37		
~~This agreeth also with~~		3.96	
as the day increased	38		
~~as the night increased~~		3.94–95	
as the night increased			396.41
shorten the honour of their nation	39		
~~shorten the honour~~		3.94	

Quotation	Page	NS	Ulysses
shorten the honour of her guard			392.12
in the mean season	39		
in the mean seasons		3.94	
Richard Hakluyt, Frobisher's Second Voyage			
a gentleman of my Lord of			
Warwick's	42		
~~scholar of my lord of—~~		3.93	
scholar of my lady of Mercy			397.24
licensed...to on shore	42		
licensed to—		3.92	
reclaimed them to their houses	43		
~~reclaimed him,~~ used him		3.93	
they reclaimed the churl			392.16–17
we tasted cold storm	45		
~~tasted storms~~		3.102	
tasted the rumour of that storm			394.41–42
to countervail the same	46		
~~countervail the same~~		3.97	
deliverly escaped	46		
~~deliverly escaped~~		3.97	
deliverly he scaped their questions			390.21–22
paganry and infidelity	48		
~~paganry~~		3.98	
his hellprate and paganry			394.37
Our general certain days	49		
~~the capt. certain days,~~		3.99	
our master and his mate, who			
coasting ..., they perceived	49		
~~who coasting ....he...~~		3.99	
John Florio, The Story of Androdus and the Lion			
it so fortuned	52		
~~it so fortuned~~		3.100	
if it so fortuned him			389.31
wishly	52		
~~wishly~~		3.100	
he had eyed wishly			398.35
blandishments	53		
~~blandishments~~		3.100	
with menace of blandishments			392.17–18
to enter-shew	53		
~~intershow~~		3.101	
all intershowed it too			392.35
seldom-seen an accident	53		
~~so seldom seen an accident~~		3.103	
so seldom seen an accident			390.19–20

Sir Philip Sidney, A Stag Hunt

Quotation	Page	NS	Ulysses
he disdained all chamber delights	55		
Chamber delights		3.89	
in delights amorous			393.16
prevent him	55		
prevent him		3.89	
he leaves to do the effect	55		
leaves to (be) do (ne)		3.89	
beguiled the time's haste	55		
the time's haste		3.90	
time's ruins			391.18?
the time's occasion			392.24
the wind's advertisement	56		
the wind's advertisement		3.90	

Richard Hooker, On Reason

both to be, and to be a rewarder	57		
both to be and to be: a rewarder		4.93	

Francis Bacon, Of Youth and Age

young men are admitted nearer to God than old [ff]	62		
memory of things in youth better than age		4.155	
the argument, which must be used, is fire; the place whence it must be fetched, heaven; the mood and figure, devotion; the conclusion, death to be overcome!	62–63		
the argument fire, the place whence heaven, the mood & figure devotion, the conclusion death to be overcome		4.95–96	

Robert Burton, The Power of Love

a proper man of person	66		
a proper man of person		4.99	
a proper man of his person			403.24
but a very ass	66		
a very ass		4.100	
he became from an idiot and a clown to be	66		
became from a clown to be		4.101	
against her sweetheart comes	67		
against her lover came		4.102	
against lord Andrew came			392.11
composed looks, composed gait, clothes, gestures, actions, all composed	67		

Quotation	Page	NS	Ulysses
composed gait, clothes, gestures, action, all composed		4.103	
coy, nice, and too curious	67		
~~nice~~		4.164	
to be polite and terse	67		
~~polite & terse~~		4.163	
slicks his hair, twirls his beard	67		
~~slicks his hair~~		4.165	

Sir Thomas Overbury, A Fair and Happy Milkmaid

being her mind is to do well	68		
~~being her mind is to do well~~		4.104	
being her mind was to have all orderly			392.10

John Selden, Truth

There never breathed that Person to whom Mankind was more beholden	71		
~~there never breathed that person to whom mankind was more beholden~~		4.105–6	
nor breathed there ever that man to whom mankind was more beholden			393.21–22

Izaak Walton, The Milkmaid and her Song

upon the teeming earth	72		
~~teeming earth~~		4.107	
teeming mothers			385.08
'twas a handsome Milkmaid	73		
~~'twas a milkmaid~~		4.107	
and sung ... mother sung	73		
~~I sung~~		4.108	
while clerks sung			392.42–393.01
I use to sell none	73		
I use to sell none		4.108	

John Earle, A Child

and tice him on	75		
~~tice him~~		4.108	
whither she ticed them			396.12
a young prentice	75		
prentice		4.109	

John Earle, An Antiquary

Beggars cozen him	76		
~~cozen~~		4.109	
cozening dames and damsels			400.19

Quotation	Page	NS	Ulysses
Owen Feltham, A Dutch House			
No question but a true emblem	76		
~~No question but~~		4.109	
No question but her name is puissant			391.24
that you were ere there	77		
that you were ere there		4.110	
Thomas Fuller, Of Jesting			
to wit-wanton it with the majesty of God	80		
~~to witwanton~~		2.140	
witwanton as the god self was angered			394.36–37
by chance medley	80		
by chance medley		2.141	
Let not thy jests, like mummy, be made of dead men's flesh	81		
like mummy (dead flesh)		2.142	
Edward Hyde, Earl of Clarendon, Execution of Montrose			
ministers came presently to insult over him	83		
~~insult over him~~		2.144	
Not to insult over him			421.39
Jeremy Taylor, On Prayer			
although the man may be, yet the prayer is not, in proper disposition	88		
though the man may be, the prayer is not, in proper		2.31	
George Savile, Marquess of Halifax, A Trimmer			
What do angry men ail, to rail so	115		
what do angry men ail to rail?		2.47	
the betraying him into such an unprincely mistake	116		
~~the betraying him.~~		2.51	
like dry flag prepared to catch at the first fire	117		
~~dry flag catch at 1st fire~~		2.48	
dry flags and faggots that would catch at first fire			396.36–37
like seed in the ground ready to sprout up on the first shower	117		
~~seed to sprout~~		2.52	
the seed won't sprout			396.31

Quotation	Page	NS	Ulysses
Samuel Pepys, The Great Plague			
Monmouth is the most skittish	122		
~~skittish~~		2.32	
a skittish heifer			397.20
look very ill, and in a sick dress, and stunk mightily	123		
~~looked v. ill and in a sick dress & stunk mightily~~		2.43–44	
fields athirst, very sadcoloured and stunk mightily			396.31–32
which put the young gentleman into a fright ..., but is now well	123		
~~which put him ... but... now~~		2.42	
(that was a papish but is now, folk say, a good Williamite)			397.13
Bloom there for a languor he had but was now better			397.26–27
Mistress Purefoy there ... but God give her soon issue			397.30–36
at nine at night all	123		
at nine at night all		2.40	
Samuel Pepys, The Great Fire			
tonight	124		
~~tonight (stanotte)~~		2.38	
having dreamed tonight			397.27
for aught I see	126		
~~for aught he knew~~		2.37	
for aught they knew			396.37
a likely man	126		
~~likely man~~		2.39	
likely brangling fellows			397.23
he home, and I to Paul's Wharf	127		
~~she home and he to Paul's~~		2.36	
he bought home and he to Andrew Horne's			397.18–19
there was a pair of Virginalls in it	127		
~~a pair of virginals~~		2.35	
concent upon the virginals			393.07
it being darkish	128		
~~darkish~~		2.46	
it being brave dry	128		
~~brave dry~~		2.34	
a brave place			396.10–02?

Daniel Defoe, The Plague: Predictions and Visions
poring continually at the

Quotation	Page	NS	Ulysses
clouds	130		
~~poring at the clouds~~		1.06	
the weatherwise poring up at them			396.42
~~coffins in the air carrying to be buried~~		1.07	
parturient in vehicle thereward carrying. . .to be received			384.24?
every one was so positive of their having seen	130		
everyone (their)		1.08	
to the life	131		
to the life		1.09	
such as I should wander and perish	131?		
~~wander thro' the world etc.~~		1.10	
who wander through the world			427.15–16
Daniel Defoe, A Quack Doctor			
I was surprised to see a skip	132		
~~skip~~		1.08	
womenfolk skipping off			397.04–05
a complete merry-andrew	132		
~~merryandrew~~		1.11	
a merryandrew			398.16
honest pickle	132		
~~honest pickle~~		1.12	
honest pickle			398.16
he began to open the design of his embassy	133		
~~open the design of his embassy~~		1.13	
was indeed the chief design of his embassy			398.36–37
for the price of a tester	133		
~~tester~~		1.11	
with a bare tester in his purse			398.25–26
You'd have burst your sides	133		
~~Burst his sides~~		1.14	
would burst their sides			398.28
every mother's son of us would be in our graves	134		
~~every mother's son~~		1.15	
every mother's son of them			398.28
this itinerant man-slayer	135		
~~itenerary:~~		1.16	
an itinerant vendor			408.34
viz.	135		
~~viz~~		1.16	

Quotation	Page	NS	Ulysses
Sir Richard Steele, Dick Estcourt: In Memoriam			
loss of so agreeable a man	146		
~~So agreeable a man~~		15.123	
so many agreeable females			402.17–18
to make his court to one part	146		
~~made his court to~~		15.124	
made court to the scholarly			403.13
my person is very little of my care	148		
person very much of his care		15.125	
still preserving the distance his circumstances obliged him to	149		
~~preserving his distance~~		15.126	
preserving his proper distance			403.34–35
Sir Richard Steele, Story of Inkle and Yarico			
a common-place talker, who, upon my entrance	150		
~~who, upon his offer,~~		15.127	
Who, upon his offer, thanked him			403.33–34
till the larum ceased of itself	150		
~~larum~~		15.128	
but for some larum in the antechamber			404.09–10
story of the Ephesian Matron	150		
~~Ephesian matron~~		15.128	
unless she were another Ephesian matron			404.22–23
(as it dwells upon my memory)	151		
~~as it dwelt upon his memory~~		15.129	
as it dwelt upon his memory			403.14–15
on the main of America	152		
~~in the main of America~~		15.130	
to recover the main of America			401.26
solicitous for his preservation	152		
~~solicitous for its preservation~~		15.131	
or by the favour of moonlight	152		
~~favour of moonlight~~		15.132	
by favour of moonlight			399.08
Joseph Addison, The Vision of Mirzah			
I fell down at his feet and wept	163?		
~~at the feet of the table~~		15.133	
came up Lenehan to the feet of the table			398.10
"What is the reason," said I	163		
~~what is the reason why~~		15.134	
asked young Stephen what was the			

Quotation	Page	NS	Ulysses
reason why			392.28-29
I here fetched a deep sigh	165		
~~I here fetched a deep sigh~~		15.135	
(and here he fetched a deep sigh)			403.37-38
Gladness grew in me upon the discovery	165		
~~Gladness grew in me~~		15.136	
Thereat mirth grew in them			392.38
suitable to the relishes and perfections of those	166		
~~suitable to the relishes~~		15.137	
suitable to their stomach			403.21
express some relish of it			401.38
camels grazing upon the sides	166		
~~grazing~~		15.138	
grazing lands			409.29?
Alexander Pope, On Dedications			
To express my notion of the thing in a word	168		
~~To express any notion of the thing~~		13.86	
to express his notion of the thing			408.16
in what places soever found	169		
~~in " place soever~~		13.84	
of what grade of life soever			402.34
upon any condition soever			408.08
tire-woman	169		
tirewoman		13.83	
upon that consideration	170		
~~upon what considerations~~		13.83	
Philip Dormer Stanhope, Earl of Chesterfield, On Passion			
The moment they felt their choler rising	172		
~~choler rising~~		13.87	
repress all motions of a rising choler			407.35
enjoin themselves an absolute silence	172		
~~enjoin themselves~~		13.88	
he had enjoined his heart			407.34-35
it is said in their behalf	172		
~~in their behalf~~		13.89	
spoke in their behalf			407.24
The most outrageous furioso	173		
~~outrageous furioso~~		13.90	

Quotation	Page	NS	Ulysses
outrageous *mots*			407.21
the peevish dotard	173		
~~dotard~~		13.92	
the mows of dotards			408.05
the late ingenious Doctor Monro	173		
~~late ingenious Dr Mould~~		13.93–94	
the late ingenious Mr Darwin			407.31
their extravagancy	173		
~~extravagancy~~		13.91	
full of extravagancies			407.19
They are, in short, overgrown children	174		
~~overgrown children~~		13.99	
as overgrown children			407.19
hurries them into testiness	174		
~~testiness~~		13.97	
their testiness			407.21
People of strong animal spirits, warm constitutions, and a cold genius	174		
~~strong animal spirits, warm constitut. & a cold genius~~		13.100–01	
their fund of strong animal spirits			407.23–24
one must have a cold constitution and a frigid genius			408.17–18
create themselves gentlemen, and are scrupulously tender of the rank and dignity	175		
~~create themselves wits~~		13.102	
To those who create themselves wits			407.39
~~scrupulously tender of rank~~		13.103	
scrupulously sensible of the proprieties			407.22–23

Samuel Johnson, A Garret and Its Tenants

Quotation	Page	NS	Ulysses
When I first cheapened my lodgings	184		
cheapen		13.89	
forced to make a precipitate retreat	184		
~~beat a retreat~~		13.89	
beat a precipitate and inglorious retreat			408.03
a short meagre man	185		
~~a short meagre man~~		13.90	

Quotation	Page	NS	Ulysses
Samuel Johnson, On Wasting Time			
you may not, by intercepting the sunshine	187		
~~by intercepting them~~		13.106	
by intercepting them			407.36
through a thousand vicissitudes of tumult and tranquility, till, having lost all, we can lose no more	187		
~~1000 vicissitudes till~~		13.107	
~~having lost all, we can lose no more~~		13.108	
through the thousand vicissitudes of existence			407.33
for such that, having lost all forbearance, can lose no more			407.42–408.01
frequently charged upon the Great	188		
~~charged upon the great~~		13.87	
upon which it is commonly charged			407.17–18
tell the freshest news	188		
~~freshest news~~		13.88	
rejoiced by this freshest news			408.18–19
David Hume, My Own Life			
it fell *dead-born from the press*	195		
feel stillborn		13.63	
deadborn child			110.05?
from the press		13.64	
I very soon recovered the blow	195		
~~recovered the blo.~~		13.65	
recover the main			401.26?
My appointments during that time made a considerable accession	195		
My appointment		13.66	
made accession		13.67	
Such is the force of natural temper, that	196		
~~such is the. . .that~~		13.68	
in my own opinion (who ought not to judge on that subject)	197		
~~My opinion (Who ought not to)~~		13.69	
his opinion (who ought not perchance to express one)			408.16–17
I was, however, I confess, discouraged	198		

Quotation	Page	NS	Ulysses
~~I was, however, I confess discouraged~~		13.70	
with tolerable, and but tolerable success	199		
~~tolerable, & but tolerable~~		13.71	
all find tolerable and but tolerable			407.38–39
never having preferred a request to one great man	199		
~~prefer a request to~~		13.72	
preferring through his nose a request to have word			408.26–27
I accepted of it	199		
~~accepted of it~~		13.73	
accepted of the invitation			402.09
resiled from their excessive civilities	200		
~~resiled from~~		13.74	
his intellects resiled from			407.22
I now reckon upon a speedy dissolution	200		
~~reckon upon a speedy dissolution~~		13.75	
he had reckoned upon a speedy delivery			408.10
I was, I say	201		
I was		13.84	
most men anywise eminent have found reason to complain of calumny	201		
~~Most men anywise eminent~~		13.85	
which most men anywise eminent have esteemed the noblest			408.41–42

Gilbert White, The Red Deer in Wolmer Forest

Quotation	Page	NS	Ulysses
white		13.49	
link in the chain of beings	201		
~~link in chain of beings~~		13.50	
that missing link of creation's chain			407.30
father, and self	210		
~~and self~~		13.51	
and self			407.34
But he farther adds	210		
~~but he farther adds~~		13.52	
It is now more than thirty years ago that	210		
~~now 30 yrs. ago that~~		13.53	
It was now for more than the middle span of our allotted			

Quotation	Page	NS	Ulysses
years			407.31-32
devoted deer...law	211		
devoted deer: law		13.54	
a most gallant scene ensued	211		
~~a most gallant scene~~		13.55	
A gallant scene in truth it made			417.28-29
to restock Waltham-chase	211		
~~Waltham chase~~		13.56	
taking a vast spring	212		
a vast spring		13.57	
Gilbert White, The House Martin			
the business of nidification	212		
nidification		13.58	
the parent birds...carry out			
what comes away from their			
young	214		
~~what comes away from~~		13.60	
the stuff that comes away from			
it			410.05
a hot stifled inn-yard	215		
hot stifled innyard		13.61	
Thus is instinct a most wonder-			
fully unequal faculty	215		
~~wonderfully unequal faculty~~		13.59	
the wonderfully unequal faculty			
of metempsychosis			408.36-37
Gilbert White's Tortoise			
to stop and withdraw from the			
brink with the readiest			
precaution	218		
~~with the readiest precaution~~		13.62	
with the readiest precaution			407.36
Sir Joshua Reynolds, Art Connoisseurs			
To those who are resolved to be			
Critics..., I would recommend			
to them to assume	226-27		
~~to those ....I would say to them~~		13.93	
To those who ... to them he would			
concede			407.39-41
To conclude:	228		
~~to revert to—to conclude~~		13.92	
To revert to Mr Bloom			407.15
To conclude			408.09

Edmund Burke, Nature of England's Hold of Her Colonies
we ought to auspicate all our

Quotation	Page	NS	Ulysses
public proceedings	236		
~~to auspicate~~		13.86	
that the issue so auspicated			408.12

Edmund Burke, Marie Antoinette and the Age of Chivalry

that she should ever be obliged to carry the sharp antidote against disgrace concealed in that bosom	237		
~~sharp antidote of disgrace~~		13.95	
the sharp antidote of experience			408.02

William Cowper, On Conversation

with much difficulty	240		
~~difficulty~~		13.97	
the difficulty			411.39
gad's bud	241		
~~Gad's bud~~		13.76	
Gad's bud			406.12
an unaccountable muskin	241		
~~unaccountable muskin~~		13.98	
some unaccountable muskin			402.21
but as I must acquaint them	242		
~~I must acquaint you~~		13.77	
I must acquaint you			408.23

Edward Gibbon, The Sports of the Emperor Commodus

his victories were not often sanguinary	244		
~~were not often bloody~~		13.78	

Edward Gibbon, Decline of the Roman Empire

By their tumultuary election	245		
~~tumultuary election~~		13.79	
their tumultuary discussions			407.20

Maria Edgeworth, An Irish Postillion

the perch tied in two places	250		
perch		13.80	
He was in his seat in a trice	251		
~~trice~~		13.81	
in a trice			403.04

Sir Walter Scott, In a Besieged Castle

it will burst anon in all its fury	252		
~~it will burst anon~~		13.82	
the event would burst anon			408.28
Foul craven...does he blench	256		
foul craven, did he blench		13.102	

Quotation	Page	NS	Ulysses
Singular, he again muttered to himself	259		
~~Singular, he again muttered to~~ himself		13.112–13	
Singular, communed the guest with himself			408.35–36
Samuel Taylor Coleridge, Scott			
Dear Sir Walter Scott... associations	261		
antiquarian (Scott)		13.104	
Robert Southey, A Love Story			
He broke his mind to me this morning	264		
~~broke her mind~~		13.112	
he broke his mind to his neighbor			408.15
clapping his hands so as to produce a sonorous token of satisfaction	265		
~~clapping her hand so as to produce a sonorous token of satisfaction~~		13.115–16	
clapping on the table so as to evoke a resonant comment of emphasis			408.23–24
Charles Lamb, New Year's Eve			
They do not willingly seek Lavinian shores	277		
They do not seek Lavinian shores		13.11	
puts me in thoughts of death	278		
~~put me in thought of~~		13.09	
I hold with the Persian	278		
~~I hold with~~		13.08	
which he never did hold with			407.40–41
goblin	279		
goblin		13.03	
Charles Lamb, Dream Children: A Reverie			
dream children		13.04	
grandame	279		
~~grandam~~		13.02	
our grandam			391.30
a great house	279?		
~~her house~~		13.07	
having us to the great house	281		
~~having us to~~		13.06	

Quotation	Page	NS	Ulysses
had too much spirit to be always pent up	282		
~~Relieve pentup~~		13.05	
to relieve the pentup feelings			409.01
Walter Savage Landor, Love Strong as Death			
I, who thought there was something worth seeing, looked in also	284		
I who...looked in		19.29	
and I know not what flowers he gathered	284		
~~I know not~~		19.30	
I know not what of arresting			422.16
Henry Hallam, Hunting, Tillage and Trade in the Middle Ages			
Reasons equally cogent	294		
~~cogent~~		19.32	
good and cogent reasons			419.32–33
Predial servitude	295		
predial		19.124	
a curtilage	296		
curtilage		19.34	
the toft	296		
~~toft~~		19.33	
tofts			396.32
march	296		
march		19.33, 124	
a pagus	296		
pagus		19.124	
William Hazlitt, Hazlitt's Visit to Coleridge and Wordsworth			
unworn heart, and untired feet	299		
unworn heart, untired feet		19.35	
but wanting that have wanted everything	299		
Wanting that (it) has wanted all		19.49	
In the outset of life	300		
~~outset~~		19.36	
at the outset			418.09
at variance with	302		
at variance with		19.40	
like his drooping weight of thought	302		
~~drooping weight of thought~~		19.50	
Art drooping under thy load			423.31
Percy Bysshe Shelley, The Coliseum			
'It is open to the blue sky?'	317		
~~it is open?~~		19.91	

Quotation	Page	NS	Ulysses
It is open!			423.09
impregnate the joy-inspiring wind	317		
~~impregnated~~		19.92	
females impregnated by delinquent rape			411.01
The air without is impregnated			423.20
to partake their immortality	318		
~~to partake it~~		19.93	
to make outlive the limits of the grave those	320		
to make outlive the grave those		19.94	
it is rare that I encounter	322		
it is rare that I encounter		19.95	

John Gibson Lockhart, Characteristics of Scott

a pretty constant interchange of entertainments	324		
~~pretty constant~~		19.97	
constant heart			418.05–06?
involuntary glances of mother-wit	324		
~~glances of motherwit~~		19.98	
a glance of motherwit helping			423.17
not so…not so	325		
not so—not so		19.99	
Mr. and Mrs. Skene	327		
~~Mr & Mrs Skene, Mr Wm M—~~		19.100	
cronies	327		
cronies		19.101	
William Allan, R.A.	327		
~~William Allan R.A.~~		19.102	
that he might cut and come again with the bolder knife	328		
~~cut & come again~~		19.103	
Cut and come again			427.01–02

Thomas Carlyle, George Fox

Perhaps the most remarkable incident in Modern History, says Teufelsdrockh	330		
~~Perhaps the greatest, says Teufelsdrock~~		19.84	
chaffering, and organing, and other racketing	331		
~~chaffering & other racketing~~		19.85	
chaffering			423.26
one continuous all-including Case	332		

Quotation	Page	NS	Ulysses
~~commodious all-including case~~ ~~(suit)~~		19.86	
allincluding most farraginous chronicle			423.26
tagrags	332?		
~~ragman~~		19.87	

Thomas Carlyle, Two Men Worthy of Honour

Two men I honour, and no third	333		
~~& no third~~		19.88	
and no botch			423.24
besoiled	333		
~~besoiled~~		19.87	
bemoiled			423.31–32
in thee too lay a god-created Form	333		
~~in thee lay a godcreated~~		19.89	
In her lay a Godframed Godgiven preformed possibility			423.27–28
Yet toil on, toil on	333		
~~toil on, labour~~		19.90	
Toil on, labour			423.29
toiling for the spiritually indispensable; not daily bread, but the bread of Life	334?		
~~particularly large & wide~~ ~~(bread)~~		19.113	
work at it, like a Hercules	335		
~~work at it, by heaven~~		19.114	
helldogs	335?		
~~bandog~~		19.115	
like a very bandog			423.29
celestial Life-essence	336		
~~life essence celestial~~		19.117	
life essence celestial			423.20–21
cleave thou to that	336		
~~cleave to~~		19.118	
Cleave to her!			423.29
on Portland-stone there	337		
~~on Dublin stone there~~		19.119	
on Dublin stone there			423.21
blessed dew-moisture	338		
~~dew moisture~~		19.120	
raindew moisture			423.20

Thomas Babington Macaulay, Death of Charles the Second

Barbara Palmer, Duchess of Cleveland, was there	340		

Quotation	Page	NS	Ulysses
~~Barbara was there~~		19.122	
Crothers was there			417.29
The learning of Vossius, the wit of Waller	341		
the learning of Vossius, the wit of		19.123	
William Makepeace Thackeray, The Battle of Waterloo			
you and I	350		
~~you and I~~		19.105	
(you and I may whisper it)			421.03
dauntless	350		
dauntless		19.106	
Amelia	351		
~~Amelia, Agnes~~		19.125	
William Makepeace Thackeray, Lady Castlewood and Her Young Worshipper			
If he joked, she smiled	351		
if he joked she smiled			
A pretty sight it was to see	352		
~~a pretty sight it was to see~~		19.109	
(a pretty sight it is to see)			420.39
kneeling reverently before the sacred book	352		
~~reverently~~		19.108	
Reverently look			420.37
~~before the sacred book~~		19.110	
read in the Sacred Book			421.24
William Makepeace Thackeray, The Duke of Marlborough			
harking his bloody war-dogs on	354		
~~harked him on~~		19.111	
They hark him on			423.09
a fond woman	354		
~~a fond woman~~		19.112	
girlish fond hands			422.23?
he used all men	354		
used all men		19.105	
A. W. Pollard, ed., *The Travels of Sir John Mandeville* (London, 1923; first printed 1900).			
Of the Devil's Head in the Valley Perilous			
that dureth nigh a four mile	185		
nigh a mile, ~~dureth~~		7.122	
Meseems it dureth overlong			387.41
treasure that there is	185		
~~treasure that there is~~		7.123	
fatness that therein is			387.18

Quotation	Page	NS	Ulysses
ne of the Christian men neither	185		
~~ne of Cristen men nor the~~		7.124	
say nay nor do her mandement ne have him in aught			386.39–40?
misbelieving men	185		
though misbelieving men nie			387.15
he would be adread	186		
~~adread~~		7.125	
that ere adread was			385.31
nighen towards him	186		
~~nighen~~		7.125	
and there nighed them			386.24
For they will first shrive them	186		
made every man to be shriven	186		
~~they shriven him~~		7.126	
with masspriest to be shriven			385.38
yet, natheless	186		
~~yet natheless~~		7.116	
natheless they are so			387.16
And thus we passed that perilous vale, and found therein gold and silver, and precious stones and rich jewels great plenty	186–87		
~~and x and y great plenty~~		7.128	
as us thought	187		
~~as him thought~~		7.127	
I trow well	187		
~~trowed well~~		7.125	
she trowed well			386.37–38
God of his grace holp us	187		
~~halp~~		7.129	
draught and halp thereto			387.27
without emcumbrance	187		
~~withouten~~		7.129	
fishes withouten heads			387.13–14
thanked be Almighty God	187		
Thanked be Almighty God			387.33–34

Sir Thomas Malory, *Le Morte d'Arthur* (New York, 1961)

Volume I

And as they rode, Arthur said, I have no sword. No force, said Merlin	44		
And as they rode, Arthur said, I have no sword. No force sd. Merlin		7.45–46	
an I may	44		

Quotation	Page	NS	Ulysses
an I may		7.42	
an they might			388.18
Sir Arthur, king	45		
~~Sir Leopold, king~~		7.47	
Sir Leopold heard			387.38
He hath ado with a knight	45		
~~had ado with~~		7.48	
they had had ado each with other			386.27–28
so that ye shall have no worship to have ado with him	45		
You shall have no worship to. . .		7.49	
they marvelled that he would jeopard his person so	46		
~~jeopard her person~~		7.50	
so jeopard her person			390.15
Volume II			
besweated	223		
besweat		2.90	
he was ware	224?		
~~he was ware~~		7.38	
And he was ware			387.41
best knight of the world	226		
~~best knight of the world one~~		2.92	
very truest knight of the world one that ever did minion service to lady gentle			388.14–15
all the door and the windows of the palace shut by themself	227		
doors shut by themself		2.96	
Then she had marvel what knight it might be	228		
~~I marvel what man (that) he is~~		2.98	
I marvel, said he, that it be not come			387.40–41
it shall so heavy me	235		
~~it shall so heavy me~~		2.68	
that him so heavied			385.34
they had ridden a two mile	237		
~~a 2 mile~~		2.71	
a fifty mile			396.30?
This shield behoveth unto no man but unto Sir Galahad	237		
~~this shield behoveth to him~~		2.64	
which behoves to the king			395.34–35
Sir Galahad heard in the leaves			

Quotation	Page	NS	Ulysses
cry on high	243		
~~Sir G. heard in the leaves cry on high~~		2.55	
Sir Leopold heard on the upfloor cry on high			387.38–39
a spear wherewith he was smitten him	320		
~~a spear wherewith he was smitten him~~		2.66	
a spear wherewith a horrible and dreadful dragon was smitten him			386.30–31
tofore that Abel was slain	320		
~~tofore~~		2.82	
the cup that stood tofore him			388.07
King Solomon did let make	322		
~~he did do make~~		2.58	
for which he did do make			386.32
full cold at the heart root	434		
heart root		2.72	
Here is I, and my brother Sir Mordred	435		
here is I and my brother (was)		2.75	
maugre thy head	440		
maugre his word			390.28?
either gave other a ring	440		
either gave other		2.100	
Leave this mourning and weeping	490		
~~Leave this weeping~~		7.51	
leave their wassailing			387.37
but my time hieth fast	490		
~~her time hied fast~~		7.52	
whose time hied fast			387.38
tell me what though there seest	490		
what though there seest		7.53	
who would have weened	491		
who would have weened		7.54	
as far into the water, as he might	491		
~~as far as he might~~		7.55	
he quaffed as far as he might			388.09–10
all they had black hoods	491		
~~all they had hoods~~		7.56	
All they bachelors			390.14
And thou were the truest lover of a sinful man that ever loved woman. And thou were the kindest man that ever struck with sword. And thou were the goodliest person			

Quotation	Page	NS	Ulysses
that ever came among press of knights. And thou was the meekest man and the gentlest that ever ate in hall among ladies.	504		
And sir Leopold that was the goodliest guest that ever sat in scholar's hall and that was the meekest man and the kindest that ever laid husband-ly hand under hen and that was the very truest knight of the world			388.11–14

Froissart's Chronicles, selected from Lord Berners' translation by Madalen Edgar M. A. (London, 1928; first published 1912).

Now let us speak of the King	27		
~~Now let us speak of~~		3.53–54	
Now let us speak of that fellowship			388.17
Sir, the commons of this your realm have sent me...But, sir, they say they will show you...sir, I have no charge	140		
~~Sir...but, sir...sir, now~~		3.53	
Murmur, sirs, is eke oft			389.20
But, gramercy, what of			389.22–23
For, sirs, he said			389.25
Then they cried all with one voice	142		
~~they all cried with one voice~~		3.58	
all cried with one acclaim			389.09

Sir Thomas Elyot, *The Boke Named the Governour,* ed. by Henry Herbert Stephen Croft (London, 1883; reprinted New York, 1967), 2 Vols.

Volume I

whan he was of his enemies embraided	34		
~~of his enemies embraided~~		3.83	
Costello was of them all embraided			392.16
or, at the leste way	35		
~~at least way~~		3.74–75	
so that at the least way			389.12–13
an auncient and sad matron	35		

Quotation	Page	NS	Ulysses
~~An ancient and sad matron~~		3.77	
an ancient and a sad matron			392.13

Sir Thomas Browne, *Religio Medici and Other Writings,* introduction by Frank L. Huntley (New York, 1951)

Hydriotaphia, Urne-Buriall

bottome of Reason	139		
~~bottom of reason~~		11.100	
a mere fetch without bottom of reason			398.07–08
conclude in a moist relentment	139		
~~moist relentment~~		11.101	
premature relentment			410.38?
fasciations and bands of death	143		
~~fasciations, bands~~		11.46	
a bed of fasciated wattles			394.16
ceremonies agreeable unto	143		
~~agreeable unto~~		11.46	
the final which is agreeable unto			394.12–13
last conclamation, and triple valediction	144		
~~conclamation~~		11.102	
conclamation of the hillcat			394.18

John Bunyan, *The Pilgrim's Progress and Grace Abounding,* ed. by James Thorpe (Boston, 1969).

A bird in the hand is worth two in the bush	108		
Bird-in-the-Hand			395.41, 396.07
Two-in-the-Bush			396.03
their original had been the dunghill	123		
his original the dunghill		2.120	
opened toward the sunrising	123		
open towards the sunrising		2.121	
any, even any	124		
any, even any		2.122	
the ox's goad	124		
~~ox's goad~~		4.09	
Parallax stalks behind and goads			414.16
to catch no slip...caught a slip	125		
catch a slip		4.11	
to question with him	126		
~~question with him~~		4.10	
I question with you			399.20–21
Wherein, O Apollyon	127		

Quotation	Page	NS	Ulysses
~~wherein, O x~~		4.12	
Wherein, O wretched company			396.23
Apollyon broke out into a grievous rage	127		
~~grievous rage~~		4.13	
in a very grievous rage			396.24
here will I spill thy soul	127		
~~spill thy soul~~		4.14	
spill their souls			396.25
Apollyon as fast made at him	128		
~~made at him~~		4.15	
they would make at her			396.09
was got to the borders	129		
~~was got to the door~~		4.16	
dangeous quag	130		
~~quag~~		4.17	
quags and tofts too			396.32
so they gave back	130		
gave back		4.18	
what he had best to do	130		
what he had best to do		4.19	
catched no hurt	132		
~~catched~~		4.30	
kirtles catched up			397.05
what a flattering tongue she had; she lay at me hard to turn aside with her	134		
she lay at him so flatteringly			396.02
carnal and fleshly content	134		
Carnal Concupiscence			396.04
he was but a word and a blow	135		
~~he was but a word and a blow~~		4.167	
he was indeed but a word and a blow			395.02–03
boldfaced Shame	136		
Shameface			396.14–15
I could not tell what to say at first	137		
could not tell what to think		4.166	
he chanced to look	138		
~~chanced to~~		4.39	
chanced against			397.14
That is it that I said	139		
~~that is it what I said~~		4.169	
This was it what all that company...lusted after			396.05–06
in his crown	140		
crown		4.170	
a very pretty man	140		

Quotation	Page	NS	Ulysses
a very pretty man		4.38	
pretty man, turn aside			396.01
This Talkative	141		
this talkative		4.172	
this talkative			403.24
cheweth the cud	142		
chew the cud		4.37	
chewing the cud			413.02
aught else but notion	145		
nought else but notion		4.121	
nought else but notion			396.10
hubbub	149		
hubbub		4.20	
a hubbub noise			395.13
hubbub of Phenomenon			395.25
for several reasons, for First,	149		
for:		4.21	
first:		4.22	
No, for he had			395.17
Indeed not for Grace was not there			395.22–23
For through that tube			395.27
for their continual abuses done by them	150		
for their abuses done by them		4.36	
for their abuses and their spillings done by them			395.25–26
So they beat them pitifully	150		
beat pitifully		4.171	
so pitifully a small thing			396.39
Ho, turn aside hither, and I will show you a thing	160		
Ho, you pretty man, turn aside hither and I will show you a brave place			395.42–396.02
the shield of faith, wherewith ye shall be able to quench all the fiery darts of the wiched	178		
a stout shield of oxengut			396.17
shield which was named Killchild			396.19–20
if I believe on him	184		
Believe-on-me			395.34
with the eyes of mine understanding	185		
the tube Understanding			395.26
ashes of a heifer	250		
heifer		4.32	
a skittish heifer			397.20
pluck up their spirits and hearten			

Quotation	Page	NS	Ulysses
one another to deny the flesh	300		
pluck up a heart of any grace			395.07–08

Daniel Defoe, *The History and Remarkable Life of the Truly Honourable Col. Jacque, Commonly Call'd Col. Jack,* ed. by Samuel Holt Monk (London, 1965)

Quotation	Page	NS	Ulysses
Son of shame	4		
~~son of shame~~		1.19	
a child of shame			413.29
pleas'd me to the life	5		
to the life		1.09	
ignorant and unteachable from a child	5		
~~ignorant from a child~~		1.21	
From a child this Frank had been a donought			398.40–41
brought myself off with my tongue	7		
~~brought himself off with his~~ tongue		1.23	
he could always bring himself off with his tongue			398.26–27
Nealing-Arches	9		
nealing		1.22	
Tale or Tidings	11		
~~tale or tidings~~		1.25	
was it poetry or a tale			398.29–30?
Kidnappers	11		
~~kidnap~~		1.26	
kidnapping a squire's heir			399.07–08
I was very earnest then to know	15		
~~was earnest to know~~		1.27	
that was earnest to know			399.13
Victuals	15		
~~victuals~~		1.28	
a mess of broken victuals			398.25
boiling Cook's	15		
~~boiling cook's~~		1.29	
boiling-cook's			398.24
Bagnio	16		
ladies of the bagnio			398.20–21
Tester	17		
~~tester~~		1.11	
a bare tester			398.25–26
gotten	17		
~~N.B.: gotten~~		1.30	
if he had but gotten			398.24
I was not big of my age	17		
~~big of my age~~		1.31	

Quotation	Page	NS	Ulysses
big of her age			397.20–21
upon the perswasions of this Lad	19		
~~upon the persuasions of~~		1.34	
on Stephen's persuasion			398.13
savourly	26		
savourly		1.32	
wishly	27		
~~wishly~~		1.33	
which he had eyed wishly			398.35
with the Clerk, who the Man that stop'd this Boy had call'd to	29		
~~with the clerk, who the man that stopped the boy had call'd to~~		1.39	
indeed, *says I,* Robin, that was his name	30		
~~Indeed says he, Robin, that was~~ his name		1.40	
Faith, no, he says, Frank (that was his name),			398.30
pushing at getting of money	40		
pushing at getting of money		1.35	
mess	41		
~~mess~~		1.27	
a mess of broken victuals			398.25
hanker'd about	42		
~~hanker about~~		1.25	
hankered about			398.18
Crimps	42		
~~crimp~~		1.41	
crimps			398.19
broad Day	43		
~~broad day~~		1.41	
till broad day			398.22
'tis all long of thy lucky news	44		
~~along of me~~		1.41	
along of the plague			398.31
what he did…How I went on	57–59		
how he did to how I went on		1.43	
having told him with an Oath	63		
~~oaths~~		1.44	
he swore with an oath			398.12
Punk	64		
~~punk~~		1.44	
a punk			398.27
run for it	70		
~~run for it~~		1.45	
Headborough	71		
~~headborough~~		2.01	
a headborough			398.41

Quotation	Page	NS	Ulysses
the headborough			399.11
was or no	71		
was or no		2.02	
Peach'd me	72		
(im)peached me		2.03	
Slept little or none	73		
slept little or none		2.04	
Watch-men	74		
~~watchman~~		2.05	
cross	77		
~~(a)cross~~		2.06	
with his hand across			399.12–13
Mr. Constable	79		
Mr. Constable		2.07	
at once or twice showing	105		
at once or twice showing		2.08	
to buy a Colours	105		
~~to buy a colour~~		2.09	
to buy a colour			401.35
Moonshining	106		
~~moonshiny~~		2.12	
by favour or moonlight			399.08?
a Sneaker of Punch	109		
a sneaker of punch		2.14	
pushed it about a pace	110		
~~pushed it about apace~~		2.15	
the Captain was the same man	114		
Captain Jack continued the same man	116		
Cap. Jack was the same man		2.16	
is this Gentleman in being	124		
is he in being		2.17	
Listed	125		
~~(en)listed~~		2.18	
list for the wars			401.36
better than ordinary	127		
better than ordinary		2.19	
Come, come, Col. *says he,* don't flatter me, I love plain Dealing	148		
~~come, come, plain dealing~~		1.36	
Come, come, says Mr Vincent, plain dealing			399.27–28
what belong'd to a Woman	186		
~~what belonged to women~~		1.42	
what belonged of women			398.16
offer'd to rise	202		
~~offered to hit~~		1.44	
offered to take			398.34

Quotation	Page	NS	Ulysses
upon the Foot of	251		
upon a foot of		2.20	

Temple Scott, ed., *The Prose Works of Jonathan Swift, D.D.* (London 1907) Vol. 11, *Polite Conversation* (pp. 195–301).

Quotation	Page	NS	Ulysses
Horace, a Roman poet	202		
~~Horace, a Roman poet~~		8.19	
the elegant Latin poet			411.29?
congratulate with my dear country	203		
~~congratulate with~~		8.20	
congratulated in the liveliest fashion with the young gentleman			404.12–13
with certain offices...and movements	205		
~~with movements~~		8.21	
to misses of quality	206		
misses of quality		8.22	
bamboozle	208		
~~bamboozle~~		8.23	
badly bamboozled			621.16
incog for *incognito*	217		
~~incog.~~		8.24	
Who are you incog?			585.17
Incog Haroun al Raschid			586.05–06
brangling disputers	220		
~~brangling disputes~~		8.24	
brangling fellows			397.23
She was at home just now; but she's not gone out yet	232		
was at home but is not gone out yet		8.25	
'tis as cheap sitting as standing	234		
~~as cheap sitting as standing~~		8.26	
'Tis as cheap sitting as standing			402.08–09
I believe your father was no glazier	235		
~~was yr father a glazier~~		8.27	
Will you have it now, or stay till you get it?	235		
~~have it now or wait till etc~~		8.28	
have it now or wait till you get it?			525.28–29
Mumchance, that was hanged for saying nothing	240		
~~Mumchance hanged for saying~~ nothing		8.30	

Quotation	Page	NS	Ulysses
To-morrow's a new day	245		
~~tomorrow's a new day~~		8.31	
tomorrow will be a new day			405.14
it came from a hot place	248		
~~comes from a hot place~~		8.32	
Came from a hot place			552.02
tell me news	254		
~~tell me news~~		8.33	
Tell us news			563.15
she's nice by name, and nice by nature	257		
~~nice by name & by nature~~		8.104	
Irish by name and Irish by nature			399.29–30
what did thought do?	261		
~~what did thought do?~~		8.105	
And you know what thought did?			477.18
if you fall by the way, don't stay to get up again	264		
~~if you fall don't wait to~~		8.106	
If you fall don't wait to get up			425.20–21
the best doctors in the world are Doctor Diet, Doctor Quiet, and Doctor Merryman	282		
~~Doctor Diet~~		3.08	
~~Quiet~~		3.09	
Doctor Diet and Doctor Quiet			423.14–15

Laurence Sterne, *A Sentimental Journey through France and Italy* (New York, 1904)

Quotation	Page	NS	Ulysses
skipping out of it	38		
~~skip~~		14.03	
skipping off			397.05
Mons. Dessein	41		
~~Monsieur Moore~~		14.04	
Monsieur Moore			405.18
complaisantly	41		
~~complacent~~		14.05	
complacent draught			404.29
I had wrote	41		
~~I had wrote~~		14.07	
her hand had wrote			404.32
a world of pains	53		
~~a world of~~		14.10	
a world of tenderness			404.33–34
cherished	61		
~~cherish~~		14.08	

Quotation	Page	NS	Ulysses
cherished			404.32
My God!	66		
~~My God!~~		14.09	
my God			404.25
put it into his bosom	67		
~~bosom~~		14.06	
opening his bosom			404.30
in his bosom			405.03
said Caution...whisper'd			
Cowardice	72		
~~whispered Caution~~		14.11	
Mr Cautious Calmer			396.22?
glided off	73		
glided		14.12	
the cause was pleading	73		
the cause was pleading		14.13	
C'est bien comique, 'tis very			
droll...*c'est bien comique,*			
said she	87		
~~*c'est bien comique...c'.c.b.c.*~~		14.14	
There wants nothing	87		
~~there wanted nothing~~ /		14.15	
There wanted nothing			404.23
Lord!	97		
Lord!		14.16	
clapping my hands cheerily	98		
~~clapping hands~~		14.17	
clapping hand to his forehead			405.13–14
~~cheerily~~		14.18	
said he cheerily			404.21
I popp'd upon Smelfungus	99		
~~popped~~		14.19	
out popped a locket			404.30–31
I declare	98		
~~I declare~~		14.20	
I declare			404.40
Peace be to them!	100		
Peace be to her		14.21	
if it is to be found; but			
heaven itself, was it possible			
to get there	100		
~~was it possible (if it were)~~		14.22	
was I left			404.24?
That I do most sadly	103		
~~that I do most sadly (want)~~		14.23	
La Fleur, who stood waiting			
without...came in	195		
~~La Fleur...came in~~		14.24	
he retired *à ses terres*	110		

Quotation	Page	NS	Ulysses
~~he retired *à ses terres*~~		14.25	
retired with a profound bow			406.04
Psha! said I	110		
~~Pshaw! said he~~		14.26	
Pshaw, I tell thee			423.37
coxcomb	116		
~~coxcomb~~		14.27	
coxcomb			405.07
desire the landlord to come in	119		
~~desire the landlord to~~		14.28	
having desired his visavis ...to pass			404.14–15
he wiped his eyes	119		
~~wiped his eyes~~		14.29	
he wiped his eye			405.03
Just Heaven!	128		
~~Just Heavens!~~		14.09	
gracious heaven			404.24
putting the remains of a crust into his wallet	139		
took the crust of bread out of his wallet again	139		
~~crust and wallet~~		14.30	
was I left with but a crust in my wallet			404.24
to bless him with three sons	140		
~~bless him with 3 sons~~		14.31	
so amiable a creature will bless with her favours			405.01
I had broke the clue	146		
clue		14.32	
I look'd at the picture she had tied in a black ribband about my neck	153		
~~picture in black ribbon~~		14.33	
a locket that hung from a silk riband that very picture			404.31–32
kneeling down upon the ground	154		
~~kneeling down upon the ground~~		14.34	
to kneel down upon the ground			404.26
treated him with a cup or two	157		
~~treated him with~~		14.35	
treat him with a cup of it			404.20–21
with a thousand compliments	158		
~~mille compliments~~		14.86	
et mille compliments			404.21–22
en egards vis à vis d'une femme	159		
desired his visavis			404.14–15
quit the field	169		

Quotation	Page	NS	Ulysses
~~quit the field~~		14.69	
to quit the field			404.40
seek — seek some winding alley	170		
seek, seek...		14.70	
Très volontiers: most willingly	179		
~~*très volontiers,* most w—~~		14.71	
have the goodness	179?		
I was obliged to her	181?		
have the complaisance	182?		
~~have the obligingness~~		14.72	
have the obligingness			404.15
Would to heaven!	183?		
~~Would to God~~		14.73	
Would to God			405.10
hand her to her coach	202		
~~hand her to her coach~~		14.74	
I handed her to her tilbury			405.37–38
Tut!	226		
~~tut~~		14.75	
Tut, Tut!			405.17
Poo!	233		
~~pooh~~		14.75	
Pooh!			405.25
Mercy on the gouty!	239		
~~Mercy on the gouty!~~		14.76	
Mercy on the luckless!			415.35
Beshrew the *sombre* pencil	240		
~~beshrew~~		14.77	
But beshrew me			405.13
in the hey-day	240		
~~heyday~~		14.78	
in the heyday			405.07
the swain	242		
~~swain~~		14.79	
the simple swain			405.06
my heart began to bleed	246		
~~heart begins to bleed~~		14.80	
of a sedate look	265		
~~of a sedate look~~		14.81	
of a sedate look			392.13
affected	265		
~~affecting (ed)~~		14.82	
at that affecting instant			404.35
conjectures	277		
conjecture	279		
a conjecture	291		
~~conjecture~~		14.83	
all were conjecturing			406.02
crying for my pains	279		

Quotation	Page	NS	Ulysses
for his pains		14.87	
(blushing at the idea he had excited in me)	280		
~~(blushing)~~		14.88	
(blushing piquantly...butterflies)			405.30–32
justiciaries	297		
~~justiciary~~		14.88	
the justiciary			399.03
A polish'd nation	302		
~~polished~~		14.78	
the polished coxcomb			405.06–07
my brains	320		
my brains		14.89	
to do the same by	343		
to do the same by		14.91	
gone off by damps	344		
gone off by damps		14.93	
a little fume of a woman	349		
~~little fume of a woman~~		14.94	
a little fume of a fellow			404.12
a cap-full of wind	350		
~~a capful of wind~~		14.95	
a capful of light odes			415.10–11
with reason, good and cogent	350		
~~reasons good & cogent~~		14.90	
her own good and cogent reasons			419.32–33
the history of myself	353?		
his story		14.99	
Almighty Director of every event	353		
~~Almighty director of every event~~		14.96	
fiacre	362		
~~fiacre~~		14.92	
chair or coach or fiacre			397.08
with wistful disorder	387?		
~~artless disorder~~		14.97	
an artless disorder			404.37
a slight disorder			416.15?
thill-horse	399		
thillhorse		14.99	
in good earnest	399		
~~in good earnest~~		14.100	
in good earnest			405.24
rose up to meet me	400		
~~rose up to meet~~		14.101	
rise up to confront him			421.35
at the age he was then of	405		
at the age he was then of		14.102	
it wanted full two hours	410		
~~full 2 hours~~		14.103	

Quotation	Page	NS	Ulysses
Peter Cunningham, F.S.A., ed., *The Works of Oliver Goldsmith* (New York and London, 1900) 12 Vols.			
Volume III			
Citizen of the World, Letter IV			
he applied the goblet to his lips	104		
~~approached the goblet~~		14.52	
approached the goblet to his lips			404.28–29
Letter V			
what turn these debates may take, time only can discover	108		
What...time only can discover		14.64	
royal exercitation	110		
~~royal exercitation~~		14.55	
her noble exercitations			406.35
We are positive when we say	110		
~~we are positive when we say~~		14.56–57	
I am positive when I say			406.33
Letter IX			
debauching young virgins	118		
~~debauching~~		14.53	
a party of debauchees			406.05–06
and who to please the ladies almost becomes himself a lady	119		
~~ladylike man~~		14.51	
womanish simper [Mulligan's behavior?]			406.17
[Crothers' behavior?]			404?
Letter X			
the bonzes	122		
~~bonze~~		14.54	
vilest bonzes			402.19
Letter XI			
furnishing out new inlets to happiness	125?		
~~multiply the inlets to happiness~~		15.72	
multiply the inlets to happiness			402.21–22
Letter XIII			
how does pride attend the puny child of dust even to the grave	129		
~~dust~~		14.47	
~~puny child of clay~~		14.48	
a puny child of clay			406.39–40
a glorious incentive	130		

Quotation	Page	NS	Ulysses
~~glorious incentive~~		14.50	
glorious incentive			406.36
revile the living	132		
~~revile the living~~		14.51	
revile an ennobling profession			406.31
Letter XIV			
Bless me!	135		
~~Bless me!~~		14.53	
Bless me			406.20
born so far from home	135		
born so far from home		14.52	
Letter XVIII			
one perpetual anastomosis	148		
~~perpetual anastomosis~~		14.54	
successive anastomosis			391.31
"I want patience," interrupted I;			
"what!..."	152–53		
~~I want patience...what?~~		14.56	
I want patience, said he			406.29–30
What?			406.37
Volume V			
Essay XVI, Asem the Man-Hater			
O Alla!	218		
~~Allah~~		14.64	
May Allah			427.37
put a period to his anxiety	218		
~~put a period to his life~~		14.59	
put a period to the sufferings			406.27
not less severe than beautiful	222		
~~Not less severe than beautiful~~		14.66	
not less severe than beautiful			406.07
Essay XIX, A Reverie at the Boar's Head Tavern in Eastcheap			
a cloud of witnesses	239		
~~a cloud of witnesses~~		14.62	
a cloud of witnesses			406.34
The Deserted Village			
~~deserted village~~		16.68	
And the loud laugh that spoke			
the vacant mind	1.122		
'Tis the loud laugh bespeaks			
the vacant mind			567.23–24
shall repair	1.241?		
~~repaired to~~		14.65	
repaired to			407.03

Quotation	Page	NS	Ulysses
luckless	1.334?		
~~luckless~~		14.55	
luckless			405.24
luckless			415.35

John Wade, ed., *The Letters of Junius* (London, 1902), 2 Vols.

Volume I
Dedication tot the English Nation

The fee-simple is in US	88		
~~fee simple~~		16.49	
in fee simple			402.28

Letter VIII, to the Duke of Grafton

Now, my Lord, let me ask you...?			
Have you quite forgotten...?			
Or is it to murderers only....	141		
~~let me ask you~~		16.01	
~~Have you quite forgotten? or is it?~~		16.02	
let it be asked			409.04
Has he forgotten this			409.13
Or is it that from being			409.14

Letter IX, to the Duke of Grafton

Sir James Lowther lord paramount	142		
~~lord paramount~~		16.03	
lord paramount			409.07
certain doubts in the royal breast	143		
~~doubts in the marital breast~~		16.04	
marital breast is the repository			403.39–40
Remember, my Lord	143		
~~Remember~~		16.05	

Letter XI, to the Duke of Grafton

in the arms of *faded beauty*	148		
~~arms of faded beauty~~		16.06	
some faded beauty			409.41

Letter XII, to the Duke of Grafton

deluded prince	158		
~~a deluder~~		16.08	
a deluder of others			409.14
engrossed the whole of your attention	161		
~~engross attention~~		16.15	
doctrines that now engross him			409.39

Letter XIII, to the Printer of the Public Advertiser

Quotation	Page	NS	Ulysses
Mr. Wilke's morals	162		
~~morals~~		16.16	
a censor of morals			409.24
exponent of morals			410.01
the opprobrium of marrying a near relation of one who had debauched his wife	163		
~~debauched his wife~~		16.17	
consort neglected and debauched			409.42
~~opprobrium~~		16.18	
an opprobrium			409.35
Letter XIV, to the Printer of the Public Advertiser			
arguments consist better with	164		
~~consist better with~~		16.19	
practice consist better with			409.38–39
vices of puberty	167		
~~reprehensible at puberty~~		16.20	
reprehensible at puberty			409.35
Letter XVIII, to Dr. William Blackstone			
Be it so	186		
~~Be it so~~		16.24	
then be it so			409.20
wandered from the point	188		
~~wander from the point~~		16.26	
I wander from the point			405.08–09
Letter XXIII, to the Duke of Bedford			
most profligate of mankind	213		
~~unfledged profligate~~		16.27	
unfledged profligates			409.38
rules of decorum	218		
~~decorum~~		16.27	
secrets which decorum			409.40
Which ever way he flies, the *Hue and Cry* of the country pursues him	218		
~~children cry in Holles Street~~		16.28	
The Denzille lane boys			424.24–26?
You have twice escaped, my Lord; beware of a third experiment	218?		
before thiss nobleman escapes out of hit		16.29	
Letter XXIV, Sir William Draper to Junius			
In many of the public papers	220		
~~public papers~~		16.23	

Quotation	Page	NS	Ulysses
Letter XXV, to Sir William Draper			
restore you to the Christian			
meekness	223		
restore you to health		16.22	
to restore to health			409.37
a repository	223		
repository		16.23	
repository			409.40
Letter XXVI, Sir William Draper to Junius			
If exact order, method, and true			
economy as a master of a family,			
if splendour and just magnifi-			
cence, without wild waste and			
thoughtless extravagance, may			
constitute the character of an			
avaricious man, the duke is			
guilty	226		
If...if...the duke is guilty		16.30	
Letter XXVIII, to the Public Advertiser			
a lady had paid the debt of			
gratitude...she shows a virtue			
which makes her respectable	234		
respectable lady		16.31	
a respectable lady			409.17
Letter XXX, to the Public Advertiser			
it imported him	241		
it imported him		16.31	
imported them			644.05–06?
quits his guard	242		
quit		16.32	
unfledged race of ensigns who			
infest our streets	243		
infest		16.32	
Far be it from me to insinuate the			
most distant reflection	243		
Far be it from		16.35	
Far be it from candour			409.16
the most distant reflection		16.36	
the most distant reflections			409.18
tenants at the will	244		
tenants at will		16.37	
tenant at will			409.12
Letter XXXIII, to the Duke of Grafton			
It is indeed highly your interest	250		

Quotation	Page	NS	Ulysses
~~it is indeed highly yr. interest~~		16.38	
it was indeed highly his interest			409.19–20
Letter XXXIV, to the Duke of Grafton			
He violates his second nature	252		
~~second nature~~		16.39	
is second nature			409.35
the noble colonel	252		
~~the noble colonel~~		16.40	
the noble lord			409.04
Letter XXXV, Address to the King			
a gracious, well-intentioned			
prince	256		
~~a gracious prince~~		16.44	
a gracious prince			409.05–06
lawful prerogative	266		
~~prerogative~~		16.84	
legitimate prerogative			409.22
Letter XXXVI, to the Duke of Grafton			
Unhappy man!	271		
~~unhappy man~~		16.41	
Unhappy woman			409.20–21
Where is now that firmness	272		
~~Where is now that...?~~		16.42	
Where is now that gratitude			409.07–08
misery of a ruined grazier	272		
~~grazing lands~~		16.56	
grazing lands			409.29
lords and ladies of the bedchâmber	273		
~~bedchamber~~		16.50	
bedchamber of a respectable lady			409.17
Letter XXXVIII, to the Public Advertiser			
a peevish asperity	287		
~~peevish asperity~~		16.52	
his peevish asperity			409.29–30
the ties of nature	290		
~~ties of nature~~		16.52	
oblivious of the ties of nature			409.25
Letter XXXIX, to the Public Advertiser			
reducing all the four per cents			
at once	299		
~~four per cents~~ all at once		16.54	
his four per cents			409.12–13
a sickly, stagnant water, which			
taints the atmosphere without			

Quotation	Page	NS	Ulysses
fertilizing the soil	301		
~~stagnant & ineffective~~		16.55	
stagnant, acid and inoperative			410.05–06
Letter LI, the Rev. Mr. Horne to Junius			
to dupe	363		
~~dupe~~		16.49	
his own dupe			409.15
Letter LIII, the Rev. Mr. Horne to Junius			
Junius says this! who yet	375		
~~Junius says this who~~		16.57	
He says this, . . . who did not			409.23–25
he would discharge his piece	380		
~~discharge his piece~~		16.41	
to discharge his piece			409.11
I would couch it in terms	384		
couched in terms		16.47	
retort couched in terms			409.31–32
Letter LIV, to the Public Advertiser			
dreadful battles. . .engagement	389		
engagement (battle)		16.51	
Letter LXIII, to a Barrister-at-Law			
Besides	436		
Besides		16.61	

Thomas De Quincey, *Confessions of an English Opium Eater and Other Writings,* ed. by Aileen Ward (New York, 1966).

being suddenly seized with tooth ache, . . .I awoke with excru- ciating rheumatic pains	59		
toothache-rheumatism		15.03	
[wine and opium are compared]	62–63		
opium ≤ wine		15.12	
God smote Savannah-la-Mar	197		
God smote Savannah la Mar		15.114	
and his voice swelled	199		
(& his voice swelled)		15.115	
[mail coach threatens collision with small gig]	263–66		
coach & gig		15.18	
averted signs	267		
averted signs		15.07	
a fairy pinnace. . .an English three decker	268		
ship & pinnace		15.19	

Quotation	Page	NS	Ulysses
sat mighty mists	269		
Sat mighty mists		15.08	
in extremity of haste	269		
in extremity of haste		15.09	
lamps, dying or sickening	271		
sickening lamps		15.10	
purple granite	272		
purple granite		15.11	
like a purple stain	272		
1) stains		15.20	
trembled through many changes, growing into terraces	272		
2) trembled into terraces		15.21	
we were entering its suburbs	272		
3) we enter suburbs		15.22	
I looked back for seventy leagues	274		
70 leagues		15.23	
with the secret word riding before thee	275		
~~the secret word~~		15.24	
utterance of the Word			422.42?

Walter Savage Landor, *Imaginary Conversations,* selected by Ernest de Selincourt (London, 1914).

Quotation	Page	NS	Ulysses
Epicurus, Leontion, and Ternissa			
Account to me first for your choice	74		
Account to me for—		19.39	
and this, being accompanied and followed by enjoyment, renders	75		
and this, being—, renders		19.38	
O no, Leontion	76		
~~O no, Leontion~~		19.40	
O no, Vincent			415.13–14
gentle and boisterous	81		
~~boisterous~~		19.42	
boisterous buffalo			415.33–34
what god's may they be?	82		
~~what god~~		19.41	
What rider is like him?			415.33?
Mightily	88		
~~mightily~~		19.04	
stunk mightily			396.32
I wish it may break	88		
~~I wish it may~~		19.05	
I heartily wish you may not fail			415.13
'What then,' cried Sosimenes	90		

Quotation	Page	NS	Ulysses
~~Sosimenes~~		19.06	
You have spoken first of courage	95		
~~You have spoken of~~		19.07	
You have spoken of the past			415.03
how bland art thou and refreshing	97		
~~How bland art thou and~~		19.08	
Do you not think so	101		
~~Do you not think it?~~		19.11	
Do you not think it, Stephen?			416.27
he pries into a pore	122		
~~to pry into~~		19.09	
prying into			189.10, 664.39–40
Marcellus and Hannibal			
never will she endure	136		
~~Never will she~~		19.20	
Never, by this hand, shall we behold			415.37
worth ten such	136		
~~worth ten such~~		19.21	
worth ten such			415.37
Yes, yes	136		
Yes, yes		19.22	
He expires that moment	137		
~~that moment~~		19.23	
Say you this?	138		
say you this		19.24	
I have spoken too much: let me rest	138		
I have spoken too much: let me rest		19.25	
in either case	139		
in either case		19.26	
whither	139		
whither		19.28	
Men are ready	139		
Men are ready		19.30	
why think about them	140		
~~why thinks~~		19.29	
Why think of them			415.04
I render you, for the last time, thanks	140		
I—thanks		19.32	
Henry VIII and Anne Boleyn			
greatly more	295		
~~greatly more~~		19.12	
greatly more			415.10
posies	297		

Quotation	Page	NS	Ulysses
~~posies~~		19.13	
Her posies too!			416.09
Bossuet and the Duchess de Fontanges			
knight-errant	386		
~~knight-errant~~		19.36	
knighterrant			413.24–25
Peter the Great and Alexis			
Accuse me! rebel! Accuse me!			
traitor!	404		
~~Accuse me, rebel. Accuse me~~			
traitor		19.16	
caviar, and good strong cheese	406		
good strong cheese		19.15	
Away, and bring it: scamper!	406		
~~Away! Scamper!~~		19.14	
off, scamper, the mare ran out			415.21.22
Lord Colerane, Rev. Mr. Bloombury and Rev. Mr. Swan			
apoplexy	443		
~~apoplexy~~		19.10	
apoplexy			396.29
General Kleber and French Officers			
one only	440?		
one only			415.31

Charles Dickens, *David Copperfield,* ed. by George
H. Ford (Boston, 1958).

Quotation	Page	NS	Ulysses
it is a weary, weary while	583		
~~weary weary while~~		20.15	
It had been a weary weary while			420.31–32
Doady	584		
~~Doady~~		20.11	
Doady			421.01, 06
with the old shake of her curls	584		
~~with the old shake of her curls~~		20.30	
with the old shake of her pretty			
head			421.08
I have remembered Who wept	585		
~~I remembered Who wept~~		20.20	
very, very much	585		
very happy	585		
"We have been very happy"	586		
"I was very happy, very"	586		
~~very, very happy~~		20.31	
now she was very very happy			420.34–35

Quotation	Page	NS	Ulysses
"Oh, Jip! It may be, never again!"	587		
~~O, Jip, it may never be again~~		20.32	
it may never be again			421.07–08

Thomas Carlyle, *Past and Present,* ed. by Richard D. Altick (Boston, 1965)

universal flunkeyhood of men	293		
~~flunkeyhood~~		20.72	
Sooty Hell of mutiny	294		
~~sooty hell~~		20.70	
who the sooty hell's the johnny			428.08–09
noble every soldier in it	294		
~~noble every soldier in it~~		20.71	
noble every student there			423.06

Notes

Chapter 1

1. Stuart Gilbert, ed., *Letters of James Joyce,* Vol. 1 (New York, 1966), p. 137 (hereafter referred to as *Letters* 1).

2. Richard Ellmann, ed., *Letters of James Joyce,* Vol. 2 (New York, 1966), p. 464 (hereafter referred to as *Letters* 2).

3. Frank Budgen, *James Joyce and the Making of Ulysses* (Bloomington, 1960), p. 172.

4. A. Walton Litz, *The Art of James Joyce* (London, 1961); cf. Walton Litz, "Joyce's Notes for the Last Episodes of *Ulysses,*" *Modern Fiction Studies* 4 (Spring 1958):3–20.

5. Phillip Herring, ed., *Joyce's Ulysses Notesheets in the British Museum* (Charlottesville, 1972). Herring includes broad references to Joyce's sources identified in my Ph.D. dissertation, *The Sources and Structure of the "Oxen of the Sun" Episode of James Joyce's Ulysses* (Kent State University, 1967) and, following a lead from J. S. Atherton, "The Peacock in the Oxen," *A Wake Newslitter* 7 (Oct. 1970): 77–78, specific references to William Peacock's *English Prose from Mandeville to Ruskin* (London, 1903).

6. Peter Spielberg, *James Joyce's Manuscripts and Letters at the University of Buffalo: A Catalogue* (Buffalo, 1962), pp. 42–47.

7. *Letters 1,* pp. 139–40.

8. Robert Humphrey, *Stream of Consciousness in the Modern Novel* (Berkeley and Los Angeles, 1954), p. 98.

9. Stuart Gilbert, *James Joyce's Ulysses* (New York, 1952), pp. 288–304.

10. A. M. Klein, "The Oxen of the Sun," *Here & Now* 1 (January, 1949), pp. 28–48.

11. Hugh Kenner, *Dublin's Joyce* (Boston, 1962), p. 259.

12. Ellsworth Mason, "The End of the 'Oxen of the Sun,'" *The Analyst* 10 (March 1956), p. 10.

13. J. S. Atherton, "The Oxen of the Sun," *James Joyce's Ulysses: Critical Essays,* ed. Clive Hart and David Hayman (Berkeley and Los Angeles, 1974), p. 320.

14. Weldon Thornton, *Allusions in Ulysses: An Annotated List* (Chapel Hill, 1968) and Don Gifford with Robert J. Seidman, *Notes for Joyce: An Annotation of James Joyce's Ulysses* (New York, 1974).

15. Richard M. Kain, *Fabulous Voyager* (New York, 1959), p. 30.

16. Harry Levin, *James Joyce* (Norfolk, Connecticut, 1960), p. 106.

17.   James Joyce, *Ulysses* (New York, 1961). All references to *Ulysses* will follow this standard format. References are to page and line of this edition.

Chapter 2

1.   Gilbert, p. 291.

2.   Cited in Thomas S. Kuhn, *The Copernican Revolution* (New York, 1959), pp. 179–80.

3.   George Ferguson, *Signs and Symbols in Christian Art* (New York, 1961), p. 45.

4.   Ibid., p. 22.

5.   See, for example, the Plotinian reading by John Gordon in "The Multiple Journeys of 'Oxen of the Sun,'" *ELH* 46 (1979), pp. 158–72.

6.   The significance of the American language is discussed by James H. Maddox in *Joyce's Ulysses and the Assault upon Character* (New Brunswick, 1978), pp. 181–82.

7.   Joseph Campbell and Henry Morton Robinson, *A Skeleton Key to Finnegans Wake* (New York, 1961), pp. 193–96; Campbell and Robinson also discuss the symbolism in *Finnegans Wake* of America as the new world, p. 196, n. 73.

8.   For this identification, as for most of the others in this chapter, I am indebted to Weldon Thornton's *Allusions in Ulysses* (Chapel Hill, 1968).

9.   Richard Ellman, *James Joyce* (New York, 1959), p. 212.

10.   James Joyce, *Exiles* (New York, 1961), p. 34.

11.   Ellman, p. 374.

12.   Herring, Oxen 8, Line 91. Subsequent references to the notesheets will be indicated in parentheses in the text and will be indicated by the abbreviation "NS" followed by the page and line number adopted by Herring.

13.   James Joyce, *A Portrait of the Artist as a Young Man* (New York, 1964), p. 214, line 23. Subsequent references to this edition will be included in parentheses in the text and will be indicated by the abbreviation *P* followed by the page and line number.

14.   For Stephen's use of the Roman Catholic liturgy in this chapter see Ruth Bauerle, "A Sober Drunken Speech: Stephen's Parodies in 'The Oxen of the Sun,'" *James Joyce Quarterly* 5 (Fall 1967), pp. 40–46. Robert Boyle, S. J., discusses Stephen's terminology in "Miracle in Black Ink: A Glance at Joyce's Use of His Eucharistic Image," *James Joyce Quarterly* 10 (Fall 1972), pp. 48–51.

15.   Frances Motz Boldereff, in *A Blakean Translation of Joyce's Circe* (Woodward, Pennsylvania, 1965), pp. 38, 141, suggests that Stephen has really published a song.

16.   Ellman, p. 278.

17.   Francis Beaumont and John Fletcher, *The Maid's Tragedy,* I, ii, ll. 130–37; in Hazelton Spencer, *Elizabethan Plays* (Boston, 1933), p. 847.

18.   Aubrey's *Brief Lives,* ed. Oliver Lawson Dick (Ann Arbor, 1957), p. 21; cited in Thornton.

19.   *Letters* 1, p. 64.

20. *Aristotle's Master-Piece: or the Secrets of Generation* (London, 1704), pp. 49–51. I quote at length from this curiosity because it is much less available today than in Bloom's time. Since "Aristotle" is somewhat inconsistent in his spelling, capitalization, and use of italics, I include in this footnote a *sic* to cover this and all subsequent excerpts from his work.

21. William Walcott discusses this and other examples of *participation mystique* and synchronicity in "Notes by a Jungian Analyst on Dreams in *Ulysses,*" *James Joyce Quarterly* 9 (Fall 1971), pp. 37–48.

22. The 1922 Paris edition reads "'Tis her ninth chick to live" (379.20).

23. James Joyce, *Dubliners* (New York, 1958), p. 50.

24. Gilbert, p. 64.

25. Ibid., p. 60.

26. "Aristotle," p. 37.

27. Ibid., pp. 17–18.

28. Charles Mills Gayley, *The Classic Myths* (Boston, 1939), pp. 68–71, 246, 252–57.

29. Mark E. Littmann and Charles A. Schweighauser, "Astronomical Allusions, Their Meaning and Purpose, in *Ulysses*" *James Joyce Quarterly* 2 (Summer 1965), pp. 240–42.

30. Ellsworth Mason and Richard Ellmann, eds., *The Critical Writings of James Joyce* (New York, 1964), pp. 238–41.

31. "Aristotle," pp. 7–8.

32. Stephen's telegram is based on a statement in George Meredith's *Ordeal of Richard Feverel* (London, 1912), p. 178. Cf. Thornton.

33. Gilbert, p. 303. Cf. Harry Blamires, *The Bloomsday Book* (London, 1966), pp. 163–64, for additional commentary on the Pentecost theme. My reading of these last pages is based, in part, on articles by Michael J. Lennon, Ellsworth Mason, and Daniel Weiss, all entitled "The End of the 'Oxen of the Sun,'" in *The Analyst* 15 (March 1958), pp. 14–16; 10 (March 1956), pp. 10–18; 9 (December 1955), pp. 1–16.

34. Stanislaus Joyce recounts a similar scene from Joyce's own life in *My Brother's Keeper* (New York, 1964), p. 249.

35. "Aristotle," p. 117.

36. Alan M. Cohn, "Joyce's Notes on the End of 'Oxen of the Sun,'" *James Joyce Quarterly* 4 (Spring, 1967), p. 194.

Chapter 3

1. Budgen, p. 216.

2. Gilbert, p. 302.

3. Idem.

4. Ibid., p. 293.

5. Stanley Sultan, *The Argument of Ulysses* (Columbus, 1964), pp. 289–90.

6. Klein, p. 29. The discussion of embryological correspondences which follows is taken from pp. 29–31 of Klein's article. Subsequent references to these pages will be included in text between parentheses.

7. Spielberg, p. 43.

8. Ibid., p. 41.

9. Ibid., pp. 42–47.

10. *Letters* 3, p. 16.

11. *Letters* 1, p. 139.

12. Kenner, p. 259.

13. Eric Partridge, *A Dictionary of Slang and Unconventional English* (New York, 1961).

14. Biological and embryological information garnered from Claude A. Villee, *Biology* (Philadelphia and London, 1962), chapters 19, 28, and 29.

15. Kenner, p. 259.

16. Gilbert, p. 304.

17. Identification of these allusions are from Thornton and *The Analyst,* nos. 9, 10.

18. For a more extensive discussion of this problem, see the articles by Daniel Weiss and Ellsworth Mason in *The Analyst,* cited above.

19. "Aristotle," p. 13.

Chapter 4

1. *Letters* 1, pp. 139–40.

2. Levin, p. 106.

3. See p. 64.

4. Robert Scholes, in *"Ulysses:* A Structuralist Perspective," *James Joyce Quarterly* 10 (Fall 1972), pp. 167–70, reaches a similar conclusion following more stringent analytical methods.

5. Levin, p. 106.

6. Budgen, p. 180.

7. Ellmann, p. 489.

8. *Letters* 1, p. 195.

9. George Saintsbury, *A History of English Prose Rhythm* (Bloomington, 1965; first published 1912), p. 465.

10. Ibid., p. 396.

11. W. Peacock, *English Prose from Mandeville to Ruskin* (London, 1903).

12. See chapter one, notes 5 and 13.

13. Peter Cunningham, F.S.A., ed., *The Works of Oliver Goldsmith* (New York and London, 1900), 3, p. 148.

14. Gilbert, pp. 292–304; Clive Hart, *James Joyce's Ulysses* (Sidney, 1968), p. 69.

15. Gilbert, p. 292.

16. Saintsbury, p. 33, gives the Old English text and his modernization in parallel columns.

17. Printed "twey" in the Paris 1922 edition (368.09) and in the Random House 1946 edition (379.05), "they" in Random House 1961 (385.10) and in Bodley Head (368.03).

18. Saintsbury, p. 32.

19. Thornton, p. 325.

20. Saintsbury, p. 64. Cf. NS, 7.95.

21. Peacock, pp. 3–5.

22. Walcott, p. 41.

23. A. W. Pollard, ed., *The Travels of Sir John Mandeville* (London, 1923; first printed 1900), pp. 185–87; Saintsbury, p. 64.

24. *Critical Writings,* p. 116.

25. Saintsbury, p. 63.

26. *Letters* 1, pp. 139–40.

27. Phillip Herring, in "More Peacock in the Oxen," *A Wake Newslitter* 8 (August, 1971), pp. 51–53, discusses this problem.

28. Saintsbury, p. 62.

29. Ibid., p. 61.

30. Ibid., p. 199. For more evidence of Browne in *Ulysses* see Stuart Hirschberg, "Sir Thomas Browne in *Ulysses,*" *Notes on Contemporary Literature* 8, ii, p. 3.

31. Sir Thomas Browne, *Religio Medici and Other Writings,* introduction by Frank L. Huntley (New York, 1951), p. 154.

32. Ibid., p. 143.

33. John Bunyan, *The Pilgrim's Progress and Grace Abounding,* ed. by James Thorpe (Boston, 1969), p. 111.

34. Ibid., p. 134.

35. Ibid., p. 160.

36. Ibid., p. 178.

37. Daniel Defoe, *The History and Remarkable Life of the Truly Honourable Col. Jacque, Commonly Call'd Col. Jack,* ed. by Samuel Holt Monk (London, 1965), title page.

38. Budgen, p. 181.

39. Joseph Prescott, ed. and trans., *Daniel Defoe by James Joyce* (Buffalo, 1964), p. 23.

40. Ellmann, p. 376.

41. Defoe, p. 7.

42. Ibid., p. 5.

43. Ibid., p. 11.

44. Gilbert, pp. 297–98.

45. Temple Scott, ed., *The Prose Works of Jonathan Swift, D.D.* (London, 1907) Vol. 11, *Polite Conversation,* p. 257 (NS, 8.104).

46. See Mackie L. Jarrell, "Joyce's Use of Swift's *Polite Conversation* in the 'Circe Episode' of *Ulysses,*" *PMLA* 72 (June, 1957), pp. 545–54.

47. Laurence Sterne, *A Sentimental Journey through France and Italy* (New York, 1904), pp. 153–54.

48. Goldsmith 3, pp. 152–53.

49. Ibid., pp. 131–32.

50. Ibid., p. 110.

51. Goldsmith 5, p. 239.

52. Goldsmith 3, p. 110.

53. Gilbert, pp. 298–99. J. S. Atherton, "Still More Peacock in the Oxen," *A Wake Newslitter* 8 (August, 1971), p. 53.

54. Peacock, pp. 226–27.

55. Ibid., p. 187.

56. Saintsbury, p. 234; Peacock, p. 199.

57. Peacock, p. 200.

58. John Wade, ed., *The Letters of Junius* (London, 1902), Vol. 1, pp. 147–48.

59. Philip J. West, "Joyce's Parody of Lamb in *Ulysses,*" *James Joyce Quarterly* 12, pp. 318–21.

60. Peacock, pp. 279–83; NS, 13.2, 4–7.

61. Thornton, p. 343.

62. Pierre Vitoux, "*Joyce et Landor dans* 'The Oxen of the Sun,'" in Louis Bonnerot, ed., *Ulysses: Cinquante Ans Apres* (Paris, 1974), pp. 204–205. Joyce did take two notesheet entries (NS, 19.29–30) several pages beyond the lines from "Aesop and Rhodope" quoted by Vitoux, but does not seem to have used them in *Ulysses.*

63. Walter Savage Landor, *Imaginary Conversations,* selected by Ernest de Selincourt (London, 1914), pp. 78, 79.

64. Ibid., pp. 79, 94.

65. The last phrase, "one only," may be from the *Conversation* entitled "General Kleber and French Officers." The general is handed a piece of paper, taken from the body of an English officer killed by a French ensign, which is marked with what the general believes is a piece of sealing-wax, but "It was no sealing-wax: it was a drop of blood; one from the heart; one only; dry, but seeming fresh." Landor, p. 440.

66. Ibid., p. 98.

67. Saintsbury, pp. 371–72.

68. Charles Dickens, *David Copperfield,* ed. by George H. Ford (Boston, 1958), pp. 583–87. Joyce also included four borrowings from Peacock's Thackeray (pp. 350–52):

"Reverently" (*U,* 420.37; NS, 19.108), "a pretty sight it is to see" (*U,* 420.39; NS, 19.109), "you and I" (*U,* 421.03; NS, 19.105), and "the Sacred Book" (*U,* 421.24, NS, 19.110).

69. Ibid., pp. 668–69.

70. Saintsbury, pp. 395–96, 399. For Joyce's early use of Ruskin, see Sidney Feshbach, "Joyce Read Ruskin," *James Joyce Quarterly* 10 (Spring, 1973), pp. 333–36.

71. Peacock, p. 333.

72. Ibid., pp. 333–34.

73. Thornton, pp. 351–56.

Bibliography

Aristotle [pseud.] *Aristotle's Master-Piece: or the Secrets of Generation.* London: Printed for W. B. & to be sold by most Booksellers in London and Westminster, 1704.

Atherton, J. S. "The Oxen of the Sun." In *James Joyce's Ulysses: Critical Essays,* edited by Clive Hart and David Hayman. Berkeley: University of California Press, 1974.

———. "The Peacock in the Oxen." *A Wake Newslitter* 7 (October 1970): 77–78.

———. "Still More Peacock in the Oxen." *A Wake Newslitter* 8 (August 1971): 53.

Aubrey, John. *Brief Lives.* Edited by Oliver Lawson Dick. Ann Arbor: University of Michigan Press, 1957.

Bauerle, Ruth. "A Sober Drunken Speech: Stephen's Parodies in 'The Oxen of the Sun.'" *James Joyce Quarterly* 5 (Fall 1967): 40–46.

Beaumont, Francis, and Fletcher, John. *The Maid's Tragedy.* In *Elizabethan Plays.* Edited by Hazelton Spencer. Boston: D. C. Heath, 1933.

Blamires, Harry. *The Bloomsday Book.* London: Methuen, 1966.

Boldereff, Frances Motz. *A Blakean Translation of Joyce's Circe.* Woodward, Pennsylvania: Classic Non-Fiction Library, 1965.

Bonheim, Helmut. *Joyce's Benefictions.* University of California Press: Berkeley and Los Angeles, 1964.

Bourchier, John, Lord Berners. *Froissart's Chronicles.* Edited by Madalen Edgar. London: George G. Harrap & Co. Ltd., 1928; first published 1912.

Boyle, Robert, S. J. "Miracle in Black Ink: A Glance at Joyce's Use of His Eucharistic Image." *James Joyce Quarterly* 10 (Fall 1972): 47–60.

Browne, Sir Thomas. *Religio Medici and Other Writings.* Introduction by Frank L. Huntley. New York: Everyman's Library, 1951.

Budgen, Frank. *James Joyce and the Making of Ulysses.* Bloomington: Indiana University Press, 1960.

Bunyan, John. *The Pilgrim's Progress and Grace Abounding.* Edited by James Thorpe. Boston: Houghton Mifflin, 1969.

Burgess, Anthony. *Joysprick: An Introduction to the Language of James Joyce.* New York: Harcourt Brace Jovanovich, 1975.

———. *Re Joyce.* New York: W.W. Norton and Company, Inc., 1965.

Campbell, Joseph, and Robinson, Henry Morton. *A Skeleton Key to Finnegans Wake.* New York: Viking, 1961.

Carlyle, Thomas. *Past and Present.* Edited by Richard D. Altick. Boston: Houghton Mifflin, 1965.

Cohn, Alan M. "Joyce's Notes on the End of 'Oxen of the Sun.'" *James Joyce Quarterly* 4 (Spring 1967): 194–201.

Defoe, Daniel. *The History and Remarkable Life of the Truly Honourable Col. Jacque, Commonly Call'd Col. Jack.* Edited by Samuel Holt Monk. London: Oxford University Press, 1965.

De Quincey, Thomas. *Confessions of an English Opium Eater and Other Writings*. Edited by Aileen Ward. New York: New American Library, 1966.

Dickens, Charles. *David Copperfield*. Edited by George H. Ford. Boston: Houghton Mifflin, 1958.

Ellmann, Richard. *James Joyce*. New York: Oxford University Press, 1959.

Ellmann, Richard. *Ulysses on the Liffey*. New York: Oxford University Press, 1972.

Elyot, Sir Thomas. *The Boke Named the Governour*. Edited by Henry Herbert Stephen Croft. New York: Burt Franklin, 1967; first published London, 1883.

Ferguson, George. *Signs and Symbols in Christian Art*. New York: Oxford University Press, 1961.

Feshbach, Sidney. "Joyce Read Ruskin." *James Joyce Quarterly* 10 (Spring 1973): 333–36.

French, Marilyn. *The Book as World: James Joyce's* Ulysses. Cambridge, Massachusetts: Harvard University Press, 1976.

Fuzier, Jean. "Cape Horn Revisited: An Exploration of Joyce's Use of Some Limericks." *Cahiers Victoriens et Edouardiens* 14 (October 1981): 111–121.

Gayley, Charles Mills. *The Classic Myths*. Boston: Ginn and Company, 1939.

Gifford, Don, with Seidman, Robert J. *Notes for Joyce: An Annotation of James Joyce's* Ulysses. New York: E. P. Dutton, 1974.

Gilbert, Stuart. *James Joyce's Ulysses*. New York: Knopf, 1952.

Goldsmith, Oliver. *The Works of Oliver Goldsmith*. Edited by Peter Cunningham, F.S.A. 12 vols. New York and London: Harper & Brothers, 1900.

Gordon, John. "The Multiple Journeys of 'Oxen of the sun,' " *ELH* 46 (1979): 158–72.

Groden, Michael. *Ulysses in Progress*. Princeton University Press: Princeton, New Jersey, 1977.

Hart, Clive. *James Joyce's Ulysses*. Sydney: Sydney University Press, 1968.

Hayman, David. Ulysses: *The Mechanics of Meaning*. Madison: The University of Wisconsin Press, 1982.

Henke, Suzette A. *Joyce's Moraculous Sindbook: A Study of* Ulysses. Columbus: Ohio State University Press, 1978.

Herring, Phillip F., ed. *Joyce's Notes and Early Drafts for Ulysses: Selections from the Buffalo Collection*. Charlottesville: University Press of Virginia, 1975.

———. *Joyce's Ulysses Notesheets in the British Museum*. Charlottesville: University Press of Virginia, 1972.

———. "More Peacock in the Oxen." *A Wake Newslitter* 8 (August 1971): 51–53.

———. "*Ulysses* Notebook VIII.A$_5$ at Buffalo." *Studies in Bibliography* 22 (1969): 287–310.

Hirschberg, Stuart. "Sir Thomas Browne in Ulysses." *Notes on Contemporary Literature* 8, ii (1978): 3.

Humphrey, Robert. *Stream of Consciousness in the Modern Novel*. Berkeley: University of California Press, 1954.

Jarrell, Mackie L. "Joyce's Use of Swift's *Polite Conversation* in the 'Circe Episode' of *Ulysses*." *PMLA* 72 (June 1957): 545–54.

Joyce, James. *A Portrait of the Artist as a Young Man*. New York: Viking, 1964.

———. *Dubliners*. New York: Viking, 1958.

———. *Exiles*. New York: Viking, 1961.

———. *Finnegans Wake*. New York: Viking, 1939.

———. *Letters of James Joyce*. Vol. 1. Edited by Stuart Gilbert. New York: Viking, 1966.

———. *Letters of James Joyce*. Vols. 2, 3. Edited by Richard Ellmann. New York: Viking, 1966.

———. *Ulysses*. London: Bodley Head, 1937.

———. *Ulysses*. New York: Random House, 1946.

———. *Ulysses*. New York: Random House, 1961.

————. *Ulysses*. Paris: Shakespeare and Company, 1922.

Joyce, Stanislaus. *My Brother's Keeper*. New York: McGraw-Hill, 1964.

Junius [pseud.] *The Letters of Junius*. 2 vols. Edited by John Wade. London: Bell and Sons, 1902.

Kadir, Djelal. "Stalking the Oxen of the Sun and Felling the Sacred Cows: Joyce's *Ulysses* and Cabrera Infante's *Three Trapped Tigers*." *Latin American Literary Review* 8 (1976): 15–22.

Kain, Richard M. *Fabulous Voyager*. New York: Viking, 1959.

Kenner, Hugh. *Dublin's Joyce*. Boston: Beacon Press, 1962.

Kenner, Hugh. *Joyce's Voices*. Berkeley: University of California Press, 1978.

Klein, A. M. "The Oxen of the Sun." *Here & Now* 1 (January 1949): 28–48.

Kuhn, Thomas S. *The Copernican Revolution*. New York: Vintage, 1959.

Landor, Walter Savage. *Imaginary Conversations*. Selected by Ernest de Selincourt. London: Oxford University Press, 1914.

Lennon, Michael J. "The End of the 'Oxen of the Sun.'" *The Analyst* 15 (March 1958): 14–16.

Levin, Harry. *James Joyce*. Norfolk, Connecticut: New Directions, 1960.

Littman, Mark E., and Schweighauser, Charles A. "Astronomical Allusions, their Meaning and Purpose, in *Ulysses*." *James Joyce Quarterly* 2 (Summer 1965): 238–246.

Litz, A. Walton. *The Art of James Joyce*. London: Oxford University Press, 1961.

————. "Joyce's Notes for the Last Episodes of *Ulysses*." *Modern Fiction Studies* 4 (Spring 1958): 3–20.

Lyons, J.B. *James Joyce and Medicine*. Dublin: The Dolmen Press, 1973.

Malory, Sir Thomas. *Le Morte d'Arthur*. Introduction by John Wilson. New York: University Books, 1961.

Mandeville, Sir John. *The Travels of Sir John Mandeville*. Edited by A. W. Pollard. London: Library of English Classics, 1923; first published 1900.

Mason, Ellsworth. "The End of the 'Oxen of the Sun.'" *The Analyst* 10 (March 1956): 10–18.

Meredith, George. *The Ordeal of Richard Feverel*. London: Constable, 1912.

Peacock, W. *English Prose from Mandeville to Ruskin*. London: Oxford University Press, 1903.

Prescott, Joseph, ed. and trans. *Daniel Defoe by James Joyce*. Buffalo: State University of New York at Buffalo, 1964.

————. *Exploring James Joyce*. Carbondale: Southern Illinois University Press, 1964.

Saintsbury, George. *A History of English Prose Rhythm*. Bloomington: Indiana University Press, 1965.

Scholes, Robert. "*Ulysses*: A Structuralist Perspective." *James Joyce Quarterly* 10 (Fall 1972): 161–71.

Seidel, Michael. *Epic Geography: James Joyce's* Ulysses. Princeton: Princeton University Press, 1976.

Spielberg, Peter. *James Joyce's Manuscripts and Letters at the University of Buffalo: A Catalogue*. Buffalo: University of Buffalo, 1962.

Sterne, Laurence. *A Sentimental Journey through France and Italy*. New York: J. F. Taylor & Company, 1904.

Sultan, Stanley. *The Argument of Ulysses*. Columbus: Ohio State University Press, 1964.

Swift, Jonathan. *A Tale of a Tub*. Edited by A. C. Guthkelch and D. Nichol Smith. London: Oxford University Press, 1958.

————. *Polite Conversation*. Edited by Temple Scott. London, 1907.

Thompson, Lawrance. *A Comic Principle in Sterne, Meredith, Joyce*. Oslo: British Institute, University of Oslo, 1954.

Thornton, Weldon. *Allusions in Ulysses.* Chapel Hill: University of North Carolina Press, 1968.

Tindall, William York. *A Reader's Guide to James Joyce.* New York: Farrar, Straus & Company, 1959.

Villee, Claude A. *Biology.* Philadelphia: W. B. Saunders, 1962.

Vitoux, Pierre. *"Joyce et Landor dans* 'The Oxen of the Sun.'" In *Ulysses: Cinquante Ans Apres,* edited by Louis Bonnerot. Paris: Didier, 1974.

Wachtel, Al. "No Cure for Oxen." *A Wake Newslitter* 14 (April 1977): 35.

Walcott, William. "Notes by a Jungian Analyst on Dreams in *Ulysses.*" *James Joyce Quarterly* 9 (Fall 1971): 37–48.

Weiss, Daniel. "The End of the 'Oxen of the Sun.'" *The Analyst* 9 (December 1955): 1–16.

West, Philip J. "Joyce's Parody of Lamb in Ulysses." *James Joyce Quarterly* 12 (Spring 1975): 318–21.

Index